Oh! in the meadow the red viburnum has stooped low,
For some reason, our glorious Ukraine is in sorrow.
But we'll take that red viburnum and we'll raise her,
And our glorious Ukraine, hey – hey, we'll make her rejoice!

From 'Oh the Red Viburnum in the Meadow'
(*Oi u Luzi Chervona Kalyna*), Ukrainian folk song

Oi u Luzi Chervona Kalyna is a patriotic march.
Originating from a seventeenth-century Cossack
song, it was the anthem of the Ukrainian Sich
Riflemen during the First World War, the Ukrainian
People's Army (1917–21), and later, members
of the Ukrainian Insurgent Army, which operated
during and after the Second World War. It has long
been associated with Ukrainian resistance; banned
during the Soviet era, it has come to prominence
again today as the unofficial anthem of the Russo–
Ukrainian war. The red viburnum (*kalyna*) is a
shrub that features frequently in Ukrainian folklore.
Its year-round beauty – with crimson berries that
remain during the winter months and circlets of
white flowers that sprout each spring – has made
it a symbol of Ukraine's cultural identity.

TREASURES *of*
UKRAINE

A NATION'S CULTURAL HERITAGE

Foreword
ANDREY KURKOV

Contributors
Andriy Puchkov
Christian Raffensperger
Diana Klochko
Maksym Yaremenko
Alisa Lozhkina
Myroslava M. Mudrak
Oleksandr Soloviev
Victoria Burlaka

With 267 illustrations

First published in the United Kingdom in 2022 by
Thames & Hudson Ltd, 181A High Holborn, London WC1V 7QX

First published in the United States of America in 2022 by
Thames & Hudson Inc., 500 Fifth Avenue, New York,
New York 10110

Reprinted 2023

For a full list of illustration credits, please see page 251

Translated by Jane Bugaeva (Chapters 5, 7, 8, Folk Art)
and Nina Murray (Chapters 1, 3, 4)

Layout by Grade Design
Map by Emily Faccini

British Library Cataloguing-in-Publication Data
A catalogue record for this book is available from
the British Library

Library of Congress Control Number 2022940569

ISBN 978-0-500-02603-8

Originated by Dexter Premedia Ltd
Printed in China by Shenzhen Reliance Printing Co. Ltd

MIX
Paper from
responsible sources
FSC
www.fsc.org   FSC® C102842

Be the first to know about our new releases,
exclusive content and author events by visiting
thamesandhudson.com
thamesandhudsonusa.com
thamesandhudson.com.au

All proceeds from this book go to PEN Ukraine to help
Ukrainian authors in need. A proportion of funds will be
diverted to support museums in Ukraine that have sustained
damage as a result of Russian bombardment, to assist them
with construction efforts and to rebuild their collections.

Established in 1989, PEN Ukraine is a Ukrainian NGO
that works to protect freedom of speech and authors' rights,
promote literature, and build international cultural
cooperation. It includes 140 Ukrainian intellectuals: writers,
journalists, scientists, translators, human-rights defenders,
and cultural managers. PEN Ukraine belongs to the network
of 146 centres of PEN International all over the world.

First and foremost, PEN Ukraine is focused on protecting
freedom of expression and authors' rights. It organizes
human-rights campaigns, initiates statements in support
of persecuted authors and advocates for high-quality
independent journalism. Furthermore, the organization
promotes Ukrainian literature at home and abroad by
founding literary prizes, festivals, and residencies, holding
poetry readings, publishing books and engaging youth in the
modern cultural environment. PEN Ukraine is co-founder
of the Vasyl Stus Prize, the Yuri Shevelov Prize, the George
Gongadze Prize, and the Drahomán Prize.

UKRAINE

front cover
**Cathedral of the
Transfiguration, Holy
Dormition Pochayiv Lavra**
Pochayiv, Ternopil Oblast
© Ksya/Dreamstime.com

back cover
Tiberii Silvashi
Painting (detail), 2000
Installation view,
Center for Contemporary
Art at the Kyiv-Mohyla
Academy, Kyiv

page 2
St George the Dragon-Slayer
Latter half of 15th century
National Art Museum
of Ukraine, Kyiv

page 5
Kolti (details)
National Museum of the
History of Ukraine, Kyiv

pages 6–7
St Volodymyr's Cathedral
Interior
Kyiv

pages 8–9
Ilya Repin
*Reply of the Zaporizhian
Cossacks*, 1893 (detail)
Oil on canvas
174 × 265 cm
Kharkiv Art Museum

Editor's note:
*'Oblast' is the name given to Ukraine's highest-level administrative
division, broadly synonymous with 'region': there are twenty-four
across the country, in addition to the cities of Kyiv and Sevastopol,
and the Autonomous Republic of Crimea.*

Contents

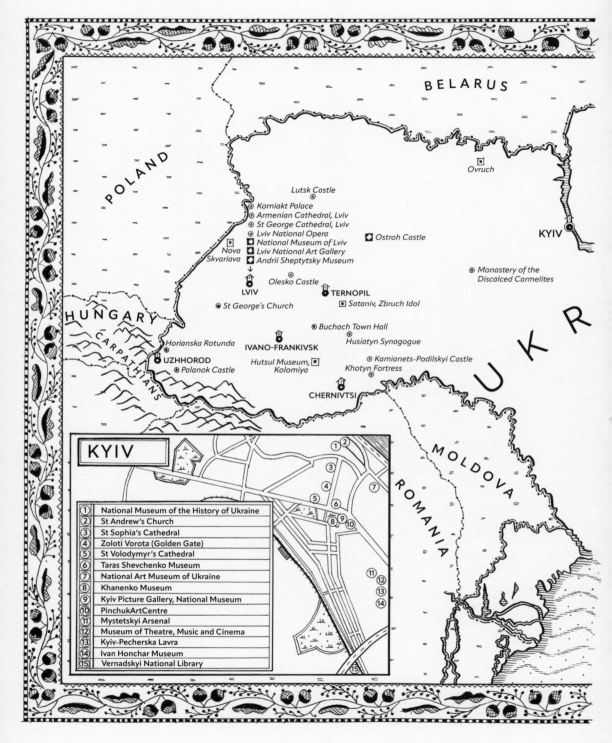

BELARUS

POLAND

Ovruch

KYIV

Lutsk Castle

Korniakt Palace
Armenian Cathedral, Lviv
St George Cathedral, Lviv
Lviv National Opera
National Museum of Lviv
Lviv National Art Gallery
Andrii Sheptytsky Museum

Nova
Skvariava

Ostroh Castle

Monastery of the
Discalced Carmelites

LVIV

Olesko Castle

TERNOPIL

St George's Church

Sataniv, Zbruch Idol

HUNGARY

CARPATHIANS

Buchach Town Hall

Husiatyn Synagogue

Horianska Rotunda

IVANO-FRANKIVSK

UZHHOROD
Palanok Castle

Hutsul Museum,
Kolomiya

Kamianets-Podilskyi Castle

Khotyn Fortress

CHERNIVTSI

U K R

MOLDOVA

ROMANIA

KYIV	
1	National Museum of the History of Ukraine
2	St Andrew's Church
3	St Sophia's Cathedral
4	Zoloti Vorota (Golden Gate)
5	St Volodymyr's Cathedral
6	Taras Shevchenko Museum
7	National Art Museum of Ukraine
8	Khanenko Museum
9	Kyiv Picture Gallery, National Museum
10	PinchukArtCentre
11	Mystetskyi Arsenal
12	Museum of Theatre, Music and Cinema
13	Kyiv-Pecherska Lavra
14	Ivan Honchar Museum
15	Vernadskyi National Library

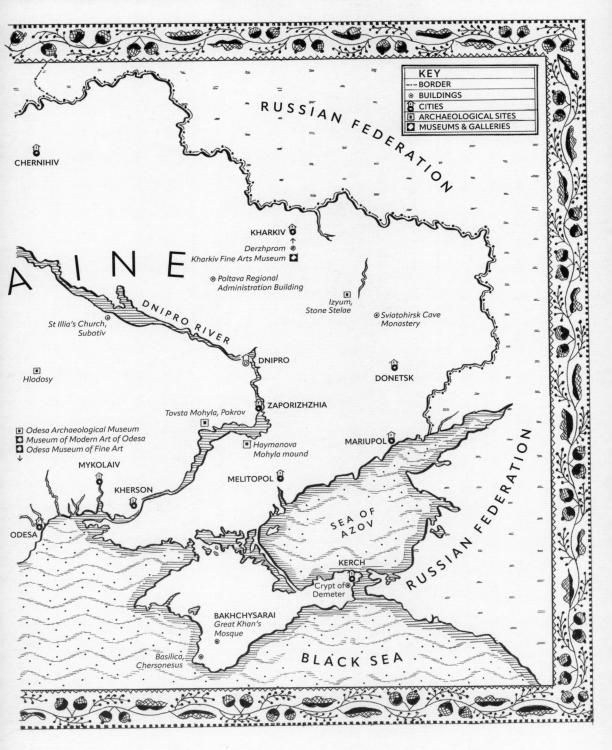

KEY
- - BORDER
◉ BUILDINGS
♙ CITIES
▣ ARCHAEOLOGICAL SITES
◪ MUSEUMS & GALLERIES

RUSSIAN FEDERATION

CHERNIHIV

A I N E

KHARKIV
Derzhprom
Kharkiv Fine Arts Museum

◉ *Poltava Regional
Administration Building*

▣ *Izyum,
Stone Stelae*

◉ *Sviatohirsk Cave
Monastery*

DNIPRO RIVER

*St Illia's Church,
Subotiv*

DNIPRO

▣ *Hlodosy*

DONETSK

ZAPORIZHZHIA

Tovsta Mohyla, Pokrov

▣ Odesa Archaeological Museum
◪ Museum of Modern Art of Odesa
◉ Odesa Museum of Fine Art

▣ *Haymanova
Mohyla mound*

MARIUPOL

MYKOLAIV

MELITOPOL

KHERSON

SEA OF
AZOV

RUSSIAN FEDERATION

ODESA

KERCH

*Crypt of
Demeter*

BAKHCHYSARAI
*Great Khan's
Mosque*
◉

*Basilica,
Chersonesus*

BLACK SEA

Foreword
by Andrey Kurkov

War always starts with words. There is nothing surprising about that; words, after all, have shaped human civilization since its earliest beginnings. But words that precede a war are used as weapons: they are chosen to humiliate and destroy the enemy – to prove it has no right to exist.

I keep remembering the first days of Russia's full-scale invasion of Ukraine, in February 2022. Not only the first explosions of Russian missiles in Ukrainian cities, but also my own attempts to understand how Russia was able to convince its citizens to commit such terrible war crimes against a neighbouring people – against Ukrainians. Could it have been achieved without words? Certainly not. Twenty years of propaganda by Russian television and political manipulators has convinced entire sections of Russian society that Ukrainians are fascists and should simply be destroyed.

The final 'death sentence' for the Ukrainian people came in the form of an article published by the Russian state news agency RIA Novosti on 3 April 2022, entitled 'What Russia Should Do with Ukraine' and written by political strategist Timofei Sergeitsev. In addition to promising that there would never again be a state called Ukraine, the editorial explained what awaited the Ukrainian people: 'denazification will inevitably also entail de-Ukrainianization – a rejection of the large-scale artificial inflation of the ethnic element in the self-identification of the population living in the territories of historical Little Russia and Novorossiia.' Thus, it was made clear that war was being waged not only to expand Russian territory, but also to completely erase Ukrainian identity and culture.

The RIA Novosti article demonstrates that in Russia, the term 'Ukrainians' is used to describe an ethnic group and not a diverse people who belong to a defined political entity – the nation of Ukraine. The reality is quite different. During Ukraine's thirty years of life post-independence, ethnic Romanians, Poles, Russians, Jews, Armenians, and Azerbaijanis have become Ukrainians. Crimean Tatars have quite deliberately become Ukrainians, many of them rejecting the annexation of their homeland by Russia in 2014 and refusing Russian passports. Ethnic Bulgarians, Moldovans, Gagauz, and Greeks living within its borders have also become Ukrainians.

Over this thirty-year period, Ukraine has developed as a political nation with a strong sense of identity. In many respects, this has been the direct result of the Kremlin's anti-Ukrainian policy. It was during the Orange Revolution of 2004 that I first became acutely aware of my personal responsibility toward the future of my country. This was a pivotal moment in my transformation from a post-Soviet Russian-speaking citizen into a representative of Ukrainian culture and Ukrainian identity – into a Ukrainian. I imagine that millions of my fellow countrymen and

opposite

All Saints Church of the Sviatohirsk Cave Monastery (Holy Mountains Lavra of the Holy Dormition)
Founded 1526; originally stone; current wooden structure rebuilt 2009 following destruction by Soviet troops in 1947; shelled by Russian forces June 2022
Sviatohirsk, Donetsk oblast

Maria Prymachenko
A Dove Has Spread Her Wings and Asks for Peace, **1982**
Gouache, fluorescent paint, paper
61.2 × 85.7 cm

women experienced the same transformation at the same time. The events of 2013–14 only strengthened and consolidated Ukrainian identity.

Since this shared sense of nationhood was formed while defending the country's interests from Russian influences, Ukrainian identity has become the natural antithesis of Russian identity. However, even without the complexities and problems of recent Russian–Ukrainian relations, there would still be a huge gulf between these countries' cultural identities because their respective mentalities are so different. Russians and Ukrainians have two distinct if related histories. From the sixteenth century, Ukrainians chose a Hetman (head of state) at Cossack gatherings, as well as senior officers for the Cossack army. During these elections, each Cossack got an equal vote. Together with other factors, these democratic practices nurtured a sense of individualism in Ukrainians and the expectation that citizens' opinions would be respected. The Ukrainian Cossacks were not weak-willed followers of their commanders, but a free people navigating complex forces originating from both within and outside their territory, the borders of which shifted constantly. This meant that in wartime and in peacetime, an anarchic streak prevailed, and has remained in Ukrainian society to this day.

Russia, meanwhile, has experienced autocratic monarchy. For centuries Russian society has been hierarchical, with any disobedience or violation severely punished. This has shaped a collective mentality among the Russian people, who are accustomed to shared, rather than individual, responsibility for their decisions and actions.

For Russians, the tsar was a symbol of stability; if one tsar was killed by conspirators or revolutionaries, loyalty and obedience simply switched to the next. There was no alternative. Historical events in Ukraine, meanwhile, had strengthened a disrespect for authority that remained after significant areas of the Ukrainian lands came under the authority of Moscow in 1654. Thus, we can start to see the seeds of contrasting priorities and values in the two countries that became more visible from the nineteenth century: whereas Ukrainians have tended to prioritize freedom, Russians have prioritized stability. The Russian Empire and the Soviet Union constantly punished Ukrainians for their individualism and for their disobedience to the tsar or the Communist Party. When, in the late 1920s and early 1930s, Ukrainian peasants refused to join collective farms and give up their cows and lands to the state, Moscow responded with mass deportations to Siberia. Later, in 1932–33, for the same resistance to functioning as a Soviet-style collective, the Kremlin punished Ukrainians with a man-made famine – the Holodomor – in which five to seven million people died. Today's brutal invasion is a continuation of Russia's attempt to subjugate Ukrainian identity.

In both tsarist and Soviet times, Moscow periodically enacted a policy of Russification that undermined the Ukrainian mentality and identity. This policy was, in part, successful. A person who forgot their native Ukrainian language and switched to the language of the empire – Russian – lost an important part of their sense of self; they were more likely to adopt collective 'Soviet' sensibilities and be initiated into the Soviet system.

But more than thirty years of independence has witnessed the return of Ukrainian values and the revival of the Ukrainian language in territories where it had been squeezed out by Russian. Today, the country's unique cultural identity has been adopted by a great number of non-Ukrainian-speaking citizens in Ukraine. As I see it, the biggest disappointment for Moscow is that most Russian-speaking Ukrainians have no warm feelings toward Russia, let alone pro-Russian political sympathies. This explains the cruelty with which the Russian army shelled the Russian-speaking cities of Kharkiv, Mariupol, and Severodonetsk. The assumption that Russian speakers would welcome the invasion troops was misguided. In Ukraine, people speak the language they are comfortable with – the one they are accustomed to speaking – and language does not determine a person's political views. As I write, a growing number of Russian-speaking Ukrainians are switching to using Ukrainian, precisely so that Moscow does not see them as potential allies in the struggle to revive a new Soviet Union or new Russian Empire. Despite the important role of the Ukrainian language in forging national identity, it is far from the only marker of cultural belonging.

There were no school holidays in the occupied territories of Ukraine in the summer of 2022. Instead, the Russian authorities decided that Ukrainian children should spend the summer months studying the Russian language, Russian literature, and Russian history. In their history textbooks – specially published for the occupied territories of Ukraine – there is no mention of the famine of 1932–33, no mention

Peresopnytsia Gospel
(detail)
1561
Volyn oblast
Vernadskyi National
Library of Ukraine, Kyiv

opposite
**Candle of Memory,
National Museum of the
Holodomor-Genocide**
2008
Kyiv

of Kyivan Rus (the term replaced, instead, with 'Rus'), and no mention of the democratic elections that took place in an independent Ukraine in the sixteenth and seventeenth centuries to choose a Hetman. Their textbooks do not even mention the name of the country: Ukraine. And, of course, there is not a word about Ukrainian identity or the country's rich cultural heritage, showcased by the artefacts, artworks, and architectural masterpieces contained within this book.

How should we respond to this? Certainly not by removing Russian history from Ukrainian schoolbooks. Instead, Ukraine should continue to develop means of teaching Ukrainian history, literature, and culture in a way that encourages individual understanding and ownership. Let us thereby ensure that no Russian political strategist could ever again think it possible to de-Ukrainianize Ukraine or to destroy the cultural identity of an entire nation.

ABOVE (*clockwise, from top left*):

Holy Apostle John the Theologian, late 19th/
early 20th century, 39.3 × 29.5 cm

Intercession of the Blessed Virgin, 19th century,
39.8 × 29.5 cm

Burning Bush, 19th century, 31.4 × 21.7 cm

Resurrection of Christ, 19th century, 39.7 × 30.6 cm

All: Middle Dnipro, Kyiv oblast
Oil on wood

OPPOSITE (*clockwise, from top left*):

Saints Harlampius and Vlasius, late 19th/
early 20th century, 52.5 × 43 cm

Annunciation, late 19th century, 39.6 × 29.2 cm

The Virgin of Pechersk, 19th/early 20th century,
36.7 × 27.5 cm

The Virgin Nurse, late 19th century, 29.5 × 22.5 cm

All: Middle Dnipro, Poltava oblast
Oil on wood

*Folk-art objects often have both artistic and practical value. Occupying a space
that is somewhere between utilitarian and purely decorative art is the icon:
an indispensable item in any Ukrainian home. See page 242.*

PREHISTORY
to
EARLY HISTORY

45,000 BCE to 9th century CE

Andriy Puchkov

T he East European plain stretches from the Carpathian Mountains in the west as far as the Urals in the east. In prehistoric times the western end of the plain was carpeted in ancient woods, reaching north to south along the Dnister, Southern Buh, and Dnipro Rivers. The rivers – wide, deep, and full of fish – flowed among virgin oak and pine forests, dotting the landscape with lakes, marshes, and tributaries. These vast spaces, inhabited by a small number of people, must have been an awe-inspiring sight. To the south, a wide strip of grassland interspersed with forest covered much of what is now southern Ukraine. This is the Pontic steppe, a name derived from *Pontos euxeinos*, or 'Hospitable Sea', as the Greeks called the Black Sea.

The first human ancestors on Ukrainian lands were the Neanderthals, who settled there sometime around 45,000 BCE. Between 25,000 and 15,000 years ago, during the late Pleistocene, groups of people began to settle in specific locations. Most items that have survived from that era, and which are now revered through reinforced glass in museums, are commonplace objects such as household utensils. Writing in the early twentieth century, Mykhailo Hrushevskyi, the great Ukrainian historian, posited that the early inhabitants of the Ukrainian lands differed from their immediate neighbours in both anthropological and socio-cultural terms, holding their own social attitudes, views on personal and familial relationships, and distinct spiritual and material cultures. Artefacts uncovered at sites across Ukraine – Mizyn on the Desna River, Molodove on the Dnister, and the Kyrylivska settlement in Kyiv – provide a glimpse of human groups that found the energy to transform themselves into specific ethnicities and cultures: by making products that were unique in style or form, one culture became distinct from another.

The fight for physical survival, of course, motivated most of these early inhabitants' activities. But alongside the tools, spear tips, and needles is evidence that they had both the resources and desire to produce decorative cultural objects, too. The mammoth tusk discovered at Kyrylivska is decorated with a web of geometric lines that resemble birds; what is this, if not a mark of early humans' desire to look to the sky rather than stare at the ground beneath their feet?

Early examples of the city-state – predating even those of Mesopotamia – include the largest and oldest urban settlements in Neolithic Europe, belonging to the late Stone Age Trypillia–Cucuteni culture. Trypillia covered a huge area of what is now western, central, and southern Ukraine; here, between the sixth and third millennia BCE, ancient people settled in their thousands before the culture declined, seemingly forgotten until it was rediscovered by archaeologists at the end of the nineteenth century. Starting from the tenth century BCE, various

page 22
Scythian gold pectoral (detail)
4th century BCE
See Fig. 6, p. 34

nomadic tribes from western Asia – first, the Cimmerians, then the Scythians, who left behind magnificent artefacts of finely worked gold, and finally, the Sarmatians – vied for control over the southern lands of present-day Ukraine. At the same time Greek colonists founded numerous settlements along the northern Black Sea coast, bringing with them lasting cultural and artistic influence. They constructed impressive architectural forms at sites including those near modern-day Odesa and Kherson, as well as along the northern Crimean coastline on the Sea of Azov, many of which survived until the fourth century CE. Even the most spectacular sites, however – Olbia, near Mykolaiv, or Chersonesus, on the outskirts of present-day Sevastopol – exhibit a limited repertoire of structures, including temples, stoas, porticoes, and theatres, generally with fixed architectural elements. These building types did not change over the centuries, so their remnants tell us only very little about cultural developments among the people that built them.

From approximately the fifth to the tenth centuries CE, various groups and tribes – including Ostrogoths, Huns, Khazars, Antes, Veneti, Sclaveni, and many others – eventually displaced and absorbed the Scythians, Sarmatians, and Romans. Gradually, out of these groups, emerged what we now refer to as the early Slavs, who later, with the advent of Christianization, came to form the kingdom of Kyivan Rus (see Chapter 2).

The worldview of the inhabitants of Ukrainian lands developed over millennia spent battling the forces of nature. Prehistoric peoples inhabited and tamed the vast steppes, where the threats of natural disasters, predators, and hostile neighbours were ubiquitous. A mild climate and a verdant natural environment of wide-open grasslands interspersed with dark forests sharpened these people's perception of the world and awakened their poetic imagination, which flourished during moments of leisure. These ancient peoples believed that animals, trees, rivers, springs, and mountains had their own souls. There were evil spirits that brought loss and misfortune, and benevolent spirits that guarded the hearth, domesticated animals, and cultivated land. Pride of place in the folk imagination was given to the bull or ox – a symbol of strength and fertility – as well as the horse, humans' loyal helpmate. The latter met with the image of the mounted warrior, the defender against hostile nomadic tribes, or with the Sun-God, who rode his chariot across the sky. In the fifth to eighth centuries CE, the influence of the Byzantine Empire brought European sensibilities into contact with those from western Asia, and these motifs from folk art began their transition into the art of the Christian era. It was a combination of cross-cultural influences that would inform Ukrainian art and culture through the centuries to come.

overleaf
Polovtsian stone stelae ('babas')
9th–3rd century
Kremenets mountain, Izium, Kharkiv oblast
(Partially detroyed 24 March 2022)

Prehistoric Times

Early humans of the late Pleistocene, at the end of the last Ice Age, lived in what is now Ukraine under conditions that were broadly similar to those across the whole of modern Europe. These people were relatively settled and relied on basic forms of hunting and gathering. The use of stone and bone, the mastery of fire, and evidence of planning in the layout of late Pleistocene settlements indicate a logical order to everyday routines. Mammoth bones and tusks constitute the first building material known to us – and one that was remarkably durable. With dwellings and materials that could last, ancient people began to consider the aesthetics of the objects they created around them. Indeed, the roots of naive realism as an art form can be seen in utilitarian artefacts recovered in the ancient forests around the Dnister, Southern Buh, and Dnipro Rivers, such as ornamented mammoth tusks unearthed at the Kyrylivska settlement, Kyiv.

The moderate climate and seemingly inexhaustible natural resources of the East European plain and the Carpathian Mountains were features that first attracted human settlement. Among the peoples that inhabited forested and semi-steppe landscapes, wood has always been an important material, used for everything from children's toys to complex temple buildings. While wooden temples, dwellings, fortifications, boats, road-pavings, and kitchenware (barrels, spoons, troughs, tubs, and kegs) are short-lived, they provided abundant opportunities for the most creative individuals of the time to exercise their artistic talents. Objects were often decorated with stylized depictions of people, especially women as symbols of fertility. The emergence of ceramics and the use of copper and bronze made everyday life easier for people at the time; by utilizing more durable materials, they also ensured that a number of designed objects, such as those found at Kamiana Mohyla near Melitopol, have been preserved as artefacts to this day, illuminating the activities of Neolithic tribes.

1
Trypillian ceramics
End of 5th–beginning
of 4th millennium BCE
Ceramic
National Museum of
the History of Ukraine, Kyiv

'The roots of naive realism as an art form can be seen in utilitarian artefacts recovered in the ancient forests around the Dnister, Southern Buh, and Dnipro Rivers, such as ornamented mammoth tusks unearthed at the Kyrylivska settlement, Kyiv.'

45,000 BCE TO 9TH CENTURY CE — ✦

During the Neolithic era, linear geometric motifs predominated among stone carvings and cave paintings, such as the depiction of a herd of wild bulls in the caves at Kamiana Mohyla, seemingly symbolic of the hunters' courage in gathering the herd. During this period – the eighth to the third millennium BCE – kinship structures began to organize human communities. The Trypillia–Cucuteni culture (often referred to as Trypillia) prospered during the late Stone Age, after the introduction of copper. Trypillian culture is characteristic of the tribes that inhabited the lands on the right shore of the Dnipro in modern Ukraine and is associated with the area known as the Ukrainian Pontic, or Black Sea, region. This culture represented a major step toward a society that depended on the cultivation of land and domesticated livestock. People of that time believed in both benevolent and evil gods, or demons, and they sculpted and carved stylized protective totems. It is evident that they also wanted to exercise aesthetic control over their surroundings as they increasingly decorated their everyday objects and weapons with schematic zoomorphic, anthropomorphic, and geometric patterns. Elements of realism, too – seen in ceramic models of buildings, miniature clay sculptures, or rope-like ornamentation

2
Trypillian painted model of a sacred building
Beginning of 4th millennium BCE
Ceramic
National Museum of the History of Ukraine, Kyiv

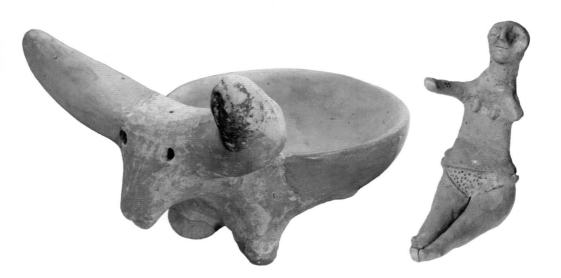

3a
Trypillian bowl with bull's head
Mid-4th millennium BCE
Ceramic
National Museum of
the History of Ukraine, Kyiv

3b
Trypillian female figurine
End of 5th–beginning
of 4th millennium BCE
Ceramic
National Museum of
the History of Ukraine, Kyiv

on painted jugs – represent a reflection of physical, environmental phenomena. Both the realistic and the abstract elements of the period's objects are remarkably artistic, and to this day contemporary artists continue to borrow from them.

With the transition to copper and bronze in the first millennium BCE, when agriculture and animal husbandry displaced earlier forms of hunting and gathering, the conditions arose for social stratification. Shepherds and farmers needed different gods and protectors to those of the early hunters and gatherers. Their settled lifestyle – and the accumulation of objects designed for convenience – demanded both protection and celebration. Art forms and designs that were by now established in the community's collective imagination continued to appear in decorated objects and were handed down from one generation to the next.

'Both the realistic and the abstract elements of the period's objects are remarkably artistic, and to this day contemporary artists continue to borrow from them.'

The Scythian-Sarmatian Era

The Bronze and Copper Ages began to see the gradual displacement of bronze daggers, spears, and scythes by tools made of iron. Between the ninth and seventh centuries BCE, the Cimmerians – a nomadic people, probably speakers of an Iranian language – came from Asia to the steppes north of the Black Sea (the southern territories of today's Ukraine). Highly mobile, reliant on wagons and yurts, the large Cimmerian population eventually assimilated with the peoples of Crimea. They were the first people in eastern Europe to be recorded in written history, by Herodotus.

Cimmerian artefacts found in Ukraine consist predominantly of burial sites and their contents (such as Vysoka Mohyla in the Zaporizhzhia oblast), which include both human and equestrian equipment. The Cimmerians' way of life revolved around war – they raided nearby lands in western Asia and Anatolia – and their designed objects were exclusively utilitarian, albeit decorated with elaborate geometric patterns made of spirals, diamonds, and squares in various combinations (such as those found at the burial site in the village of Zolne, Crimea). Monumental sculpture is represented by statues of warriors in the form of stone pillars, carved to depict details of weaponry and clothing such as belts, daggers, and battle mallets (for example, statues found at the burial site near the village of Belogradets, in today's Bulgaria).

The Scythians, a nomadic people of Iranian origin, who inhabited central Eurasia and eastern Europe, began to migrate to the lands of present-day Ukraine in the late eighth century BCE. The Scythians displaced the Cimmerians from the Ukrainian Pontic steppes and proceeded, from the beginning of the seventh to the second century BCE, to domesticate the vast space between the Danube and the Dnipro

4
Bow case (*gorytus*) with scenes from the life of Achilles
Cimmerian, 4th century BCE
Gold, 65 × 35 cm
From mound near Melitopol, Zaporizhzhia oblast
Treasury of the National Museum of the History of Ukraine, Kyiv

owl with scenes from the life
f Scythians in high relief (detail)
th century BCE
iilded silver
leight 9.7 cm; diameter 10.5 cm
rom the Haymanova Mohyla
nound, Zaporizhzhia oblast
reasury of the National Museum
f the History of Ukraine, Kyiv

Rivers, from the Black Sea shore to the marshes of today's Belarus. The geographical spread of the Scythian agricultural and herding tribes is explained by their different social organization, which also brought about the end of kin-based hierarchies. Scythian tribes formed alliances with each other and governed through a type of military democracy. This in turn led to further social and economic stratification within Scythian communities, and the separation of agriculture and craft. We can deduce the style of Scythian dwellings from their burial structures: roof-over-post constructions in forested steppe regions (like the Chyhyryn burial sites), catacombs under mounds in the lower Dnipro region (such as the fourth to third century BCE sites of Chortomlyk, Solokha, and Tovsta Mohyla), and stone chambers in Crimea.

The two main characteristics of Scythian art are the geometric ornamentation of pottery associated with the Bronze Age tradition, and the 'animal style'. Depictions of animals and birds came to dominate the ornamentation of weapons and utilitarian objects from the Dnister to southern Siberia. Artefacts in this style include not only everyday items, but also jewelry, an indication both of the wearer's status, and of the craftsperson's creativity and skill.

It seems likely that such zoomorphic expressions of artistic thought reflected a sense that another world existed next to their own: one in which animals' relationships with each other resembled those of people. Animals were depicted both in symbolic form (in which the animal represents the human) and in a way that celebrated human dominance (the human as the tamer of animals). Depictions of fauna on utilitarian objects and items of personal adornment became the central distinguishing feature of Scythian jewelry, of which the most outstanding example is the gold pectoral found at the Tovsta Mohyla mound (Fig. 6, p. 34).

This Scythian gold pectoral, weighing over a kilogram, was found in 1971 near the town of Pokrov in the Dnipropetrovsk oblast of southeastern Ukraine, near the banks of the Dnipro River. It is made up of two openwork crescents with three-dimensional figures, and a central crescent decorated with spirals, with all three framed by a border of twisted plaits. The lower, larger crescent is filled with depictions of wild predators savaging peaceful herbivores. The smaller upper section shows domestic animals and Scythians engaged in husbandry, clothes-making, and discussing the events of the day. The narratives of the bottom section are thus in complete opposition to those at the top, where peace, contentment, and serenity dominate.

By contrast to the pectoral, Scythian stone 'babas', figures placed atop mounds, convey crudely carved images of bearded men. The contrast is rather puzzling, since their creators were from the same cultural group responsible for the exquisite craftsmanship of the animal style. This mystery still challenges scholars today.

In the third century BCE, the Scythians weakened and yielded to new arrivals from the east: the Sarmatians, a people whose religious life and art were based on the cult of the horse. Gold necklaces and crystal pendants, embellished metal ceremonial belts, carnelian jewelry and glass-bead necklaces, as well as earrings and bracelets worn by Sarmatian men and women are as well crafted as Scythian objects that in their turn, had borne the imprint of Hellenic culture.

6 (*below*)
Gold pectoral
4th century BCE
Gold
Diameter 36 cm
From the Tovsta Mohyla mound,
Pokrov, Dnipropetrovsk oblast
Treasury of the National Museum
of the History of Ukraine, Kyiv

7a (*opposite, left*)
Necklace
7th–6th centuries BCE
Gold, chalcedony, glass
Pendant diameter 5.7 cm
Hlodosy, Kirovohrad oblast
Treasury of the National Museum
of the History of Ukraine, Kyiv

7b (*opposite, top right*)
**Fragment of a necklace with
pendants**
7th–6th centuries BCE
Gold, chalcedony, glass
Pendant 7.8 × 4.5 cm
Hlodosy, Kirovohrad oblast
Treasury of the National Museum
of the History of Ukraine, Kyiv

7c (*opposite, bottom right*)
**Necklace in the form of
a twisted chain**
7th–6th centuries BCE
Gold, pearl, agate
Length 60 cm; diameter
of pendant 6.5 cm
Hlodosy, Kirovohrad oblast
Treasury of the National Museum
of the History of Ukraine, Kyiv

Ancient City-States of the Pontic Region

From the end of the seventh to the sixth centuries BCE, Greek colonists founded a great number of cities and smaller settlements along the Black Sea shore, and in the lagoons and deltas created by river mouths. The art and cultural forms of ancient Greece and Rome had an important influence on Ukrainian culture. Hellenic colonies in the Ukrainian Pontic region, which were effectively independent city-states, produced settlements that were models of urban planning and rational organization. Cultural order was brought to bear on the chaos of earlier societies, and these ancient city-states succeeded in facilitating the coexistence of different peoples on the shores of the Kerch Strait (known then as the Cimmerian Bosporus), in western Crimea, and in the lower valleys of the Buh and Dnister Rivers.

In the fifth century BCE, immigrants from Heraclea Pontica founded Chersonesus (near today's Sevastopol). Black Sea city-states soon grew into important trade hubs and, with their strong ties to Greece and Rome, the Black Sea colonies became key cultural outposts. These outside influences shaped the cultural development of local multi-ethnic populations, whose own vernacular artistic traditions in turn reinterpreted locally made Hellenic objects. Agriculture (and viticulture), animal husbandry, fishing, and crafts (metalworking, pottery, bronze-casting, weaving, domestic sculpture, jewelry-making, and building) created the economic basis for urban growth both within the defensive walls and beyond them. There were hundreds of ancient rural settlements as well: excavations in the lower Buh valley, in western and eastern Crimea, and on the Taman Peninsula, have revealed remains of dwellings and fortifications, as well as auxiliary buildings and burial chambers.

Of the most important Hellenic cities, Chersonesus and Olbia have been the most extensively studied. At the peak of the Hellenic era (the fifth to third centuries BCE), all cities were dominated by an *acropolis* (the upper city), located on an elevated site, and organized around an *agora* (a public square), surrounded by amphitheatres, other public buildings, and marble monuments. Temples and altars were erected on sacred sites, called the *temene*. Residential neighbourhoods filled the rest of the space inside the city walls with common Greek-style buildings. Communities enjoyed a high standard of living, with *otium* and *negotium* (leisure and business) in a daily balance. This is evidenced by the enviable traditional Hellenic architecture (Doric and Ionic styles) used in the structural forms of both public and private buildings; individual examples of two-storey homes belonging to the Greek aristocracy, with their peristyle courtyards decorated with mosaics and frescoes; and the quality of everyday ceramics and jewelry.

8
'Basilica 1935', Chersonesus
(two views)
6th century CE
Marble
Building plan 32.5 × 18.5 m
Crimea, near Sevastopol

Among the Hellenic heritage of the area, of greatest interest to us today are the preserved mural paintings – in particular because no paintings have survived from this era in southern and western Europe. Although rooted in the Classical tradition, the murals in burial chambers also display new features associated with the existence of a local school of painting. Painters of the Cimmerian Bosporus region had their own interpretation of sacred events, depicting them, for example, using everyday details, and combining a realistic manner with ornamentation.

The Crypt of Demeter, which dates to the first century BCE and which was discovered in Kerch in 1895, is a monument of global significance. The stone-walled burial chamber is painted inside with flowers, garlands, and narrative compositions illustrating the myth of the abduction of Persephone, daughter of the Earth goddess Demeter, by Hades, the god of the underworld. The depiction of Demeter's sorrowful face on one wall, and Hades carrying away Persephone in his chariot on another, are like fragments of a film reel: the mother looks at her daughter, while Hades keeps an uneasy eye on Demeter. The earthly and the underworld, life and memory, hope and hopelessness, intersect in the tomb's paintings, emphasizing that both realistic and metaphysical views of the world are intertwined, even in such an ancient work of art.

9
Scene of the abduction of Persephone by Hades in the lunette of the Crypt of Demeter in Kerch
Floral style, early 1st century CE
Fresco
Kerch, Crimea

'The earthly and the underworld, life and memory, hope and hopelessness, intersect in the tomb's paintings, emphasizing that both realistic and metaphysical views of the world are intertwined, even in such an ancient work of art.'

Early Slavs

The early Slavs were known from the first century CE onwards, under the names of the Veneti, the Antes people, the Sclaveni, and others. Early Slavic art was closely associated with the group's beliefs, customs, and rituals, and is dominated by adornments of everyday utensils, clothes, and weapons.

The earliest Slav settlements, dating to the second and first centuries BCE, were discovered on the Pylypenkova Mountain near Kaniv (north-central Ukraine) and the village of Zarubyntsi near Pereiaslav (just south of Kyiv); these are collectively referred to as the Zarubyntsi culture. The fortified settlements are encircled by banked ditches and wooden-spike fences. The architectural forms were built from wood on stone foundations, and remains of pagan sacred sites have also been found in Kyiv. Paganism at the time was not so much a religion as a worldview – a coherent conception of the universe.

The early Slavs' artistic practice was closely intertwined with the idea of the aesthetics of everyday life. Various domestic objects, weapons, tools, and clothing were carved and embroidered; these and bronze and precious-metal jewelry were decorated with bold, unique patterns. It was in this sphere of ornamentation that the Slav craftspeople exercised their inexhaustible imagination and mastery. Pagan beliefs saw the divine in the forces of nature, and these informed the design and layout of decorative compositions, which therefore require not only their literal decoding but also the translation of their symbolic lexicon.

The design practices of the Slavs who inhabited lands along the middle Dnipro can be seen in many of the bronze objects – brooches, buckles, and earrings – decorated with colourful enamel inserts, crafted by the Cherniakhiv culture in the second to fourth centuries. There is a notable contrast between the less complex artefacts from the Zarubyntsi culture and those from the more technologically complex Cherniakhiv culture, which was not without influence from the Germanic tribes. Animalistic images on these items are stylized, but still bold and expressive (such as those from the Martynivka Treasure of the sixth century). Thin metal

'The early Slavs' artistic practice was closely intertwined with the idea of the aesthetics of everyday life.'

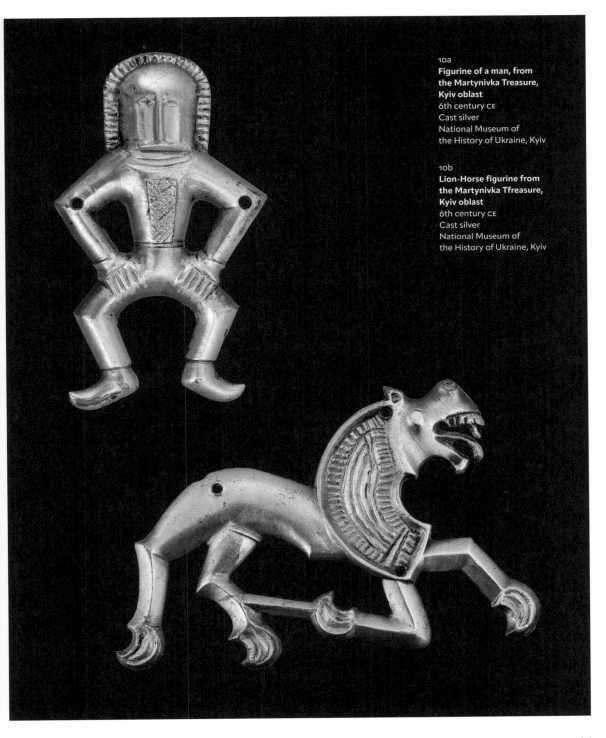

10a
Figurine of a man, from the Martynivka Treasure, Kyiv oblast
6th century CE
Cast silver
National Museum of the History of Ukraine, Kyiv

10b
Lion-Horse figurine from the Martynivka Tfreasure, Kyiv oblast
6th century CE
Cast silver
National Museum of the History of Ukraine, Kyiv

reliefs of 'dancing men', birds, and fantastic beasts, made to be detachable from cloth or leather, occur in seventh-century hoards on brooches and buckles, as well as bracelets. Many such articles involve a complex intertwining of human and animal images. This merging of the two realms – the human and the animal, which can also be seen in objects from the Scythian–Sarmatian era – may be evidence of a syncretic view the early Slavs had of themselves in a world where some creatures crawl, others leap, and yet others fly, while humans hunt or attempt to tame them, and by doing so, discover the meaning of life.

The statue known as the Zbruch Idol (dating from the seventh to ninth century CE) most fully reveals the ancient Slav worldview. The top part of the figure represents the heavens, the middle shows the Earth populated by people, and the lower part depicts an underworld full of mythological characters that support the Earth and people above. The top section features human-like figures in serene, magnificent poses, while the middle shows people who appear to be holding hands in a circle, dancing; the faces of the subterranean characters in the bottom section are angry and frightening. The images of people on the statue are all generalized and reduced to their essential features. The Zbruch Idol reliefs represent not only the Slavic pantheon but also the sacral and spatial model of the pagan world.

The numerous objects created by the early Slavs attest to the sophisticated and poetic artistic culture of these tribes, which probably made it easier for them later to adopt new Christian aesthetics – these in turn incorporated existing folkloric images and concepts.

11
Zbruch Idol
(shown from all four sides)
c. 7th–9th century CE
Limestone
Height 2.67 m
From Sataniv, on the Zbruch River, Khmelnytskyi oblast
Archaeological Museum of Kraków, Poland

'The Zbruch Idol reliefs represent not only the Slavic pantheon but also the sacral and spatial model of the pagan world.'

Byzantine Era: Icon-Painting

During the period from the fifth to the eighth century CE, Slavs (including the Sclaveni and Antes people) emerged powerfully onto the European historical arena. The Slavs of what is now Ukraine were open to two major cultural currents. The first came from the south, from the Byzantine Empire which, in the era of Justinian the Great (sixth century CE), represented the pinnacle of European culture to which other societies aspired. The second current came from Asia, and was not homogeneous, but rather a diverse mixture of different cultures – bellicose

12
Virgin with Child
Second half of the 6th century CE
Encaustic
Bohdan and Varvara Khanenko
National Museum of Arts, Kyiv

(the Huns) or more peaceful (the Syrians) – that developed at various times in different parts of Eurasia. Both Byzantine and Near Eastern influences found their way to early Ukrainians with the help of Arab and Byzantine merchants, as well as through immediate and regular encounters with the nomads of the southern Ukrainian steppes. These nomadic tribes played a significant role in dispersing Near Eastern artistic influences through the lands of present-day Ukraine, where their designs, styles, and forms mixed and cross-pollinated with Byzantine trends. Nevertheless, this did not prevent the Slavs from crossing the Danube several times in the sixth and seventh centuries and arriving at the walls of Constantinople with hostile intentions.

Social stratification, the growth of agriculture and crafts, a clear division of labour, and participation in regular trade with Byzantium and Near Eastern states combined in the Slavic world to create the requisite conditions for the manufacture of surplus goods. Individuals at the top of the social hierarchy owned these products and disposed of them for their personal benefit. These developments paved the way for the decline of early tribal society; trade links between lands along the Dnipro and the Roman Empire accelerated this process. The Slavs, unlike Byzantium, did not develop a strong centralized monarchy or a separate class of nobility, but the division of labour within these tribes produced a class of artists that stood out from the larger group of craftspeople.

Having survived the upheaval caused by the Goths – whose crusade against the Roman Empire helped bring about its downfall – the culture of the Ukrainian Pontic region did not, however, remain untouched by the disruption of the ancient world as it transformed into a Christian one. Christianity arrived in the south of Ukraine from Byzantium nearly seven hundred years before Kyiv's Christianization at the end of the tenth century. Cadmus, the bishop of Bosporus, represented a separate episcopate at the Council of Nycaea in 325 CE, although church legend claims it was first preached in Crimea and Kyiv by Andrew the Apostle in the first century CE. Of the icons painted during the period from the sixth to the eighth century, the best are those created using the encaustic technique, which Christian painters inherited from their predecessors. The icons *Virgin with Child* (Fig. 12, p. 44), *John the Baptist* (Fig. 13, p. 45), and *Saints Sergius and Bacchus* (Fig. 14), painted in Byzantium in a free, even impressionistic manner, are now in the Bohdan and Varvara Khanenko National Museum of Arts in Kyiv. The treatment of details in these works shows a living link to the art of Classical antiquity. The encaustic technique, whereby pigments are mixed with hot liquid wax, produces a multi-layered effect: the dark crimson robes of the

14
Saints Sergius and Bacchus
Late 7th–early 8th century CE
Encaustic
Bohdan and Varvara Khanenko
National Museum of Arts, Kyiv

'Nomadic tribes played a significant role in dispersing Near Eastern artistic influences through the lands of present-day Ukraine, where their designs, styles, and forms mixed and cross-pollinated with Byzantine trends.'

Virgin and Christ, combined with muted gold, gives the impression that the figures are separating from their background, moving closer to the viewer. The high standard of execution and the Byzantine style of the subjects' dress have led scholars to associate the St John icon with the Constantinople school of painting. John the Baptist's expressive face brings to mind an eastern Christian anchorite, suggesting the icon was painted by an artist from Alexandria. *Saints Sergius and Bacchus*, meanwhile, aligns with the Palestinian–Syrian type of icon painting. The subjects were especially venerated in Constantinople; they are presented in full frontal view, with bold, precise outline and vivid, expressive colours. Although *Saints Sergius and Bacchus* has more typical features of icon-painting than *Virgin with Child*, the two works both rely on the same organic use of Classical traditions, evident in the application of light and shadow, variegated tones, and an overall sensuousness far removed from the ascetic treatment of *John the Baptist*. The legacy of Classical antiquity – in addition to that of Byzantine icon-painting – would continue to inform Ukrainian art through later eras.

Ceramic jug
Early 20th century
Opishnia, Poltava oblast
Clay; engobe, watering
Height 20.4 cm

Pumpkin jug
Vasyl Shostopalets
1868
Volyn oblast
Clay; engobe, watering
Height 31.9 cm

'Twins with ear' vessel
1846
Podillia
Wood; engobe, watering
Height 21 cm

*Pottery has a long history in Ukraine. Until 1861, peasants produced decorative
and applied arts not only for personal use, but also as tribute for their landowners.
According to historical documents from 1834, a serf master potter was required to
produce 10,400 clay tiles and 15,600 pots per year in exchange for meagre wages.*

Ceramic jug
Early 20th century
Middle Dnipro, Poltava oblast
Clay; engobe, watering
Height 15.5 cm

Pot with 'ear'
20th century
Polianska village,
Zakarpattia oblast
Clay; engobe, watering
Height 19.8 cm

Over the centuries, pottery was traded in many different ways. One of the oldest was a non-monetary exchange for food. In the nineteenth century in the Poltava region, for instance, it was customary to pour as much grain as could fit into a simple pot, and then exchange the pot for that amount of grain. See page 242.

KYIVAN RUS

9th to 13th centuries

Christian Raffensperger

T he medieval history of eastern Europe is dominated by a political entity known as the kingdom of Rus, often called Kyivan Rus after its capital. It was centred on the modern Ukrainian capital, Kyiv, but its limits stretched at various times to include parts of several modern eastern European countries, including Russia, Belarus, and Poland. Kyivan Rus has its beginnings in the exploration and exploitation of the eastern European river systems by Scandinavians, often called 'Varangians' in historical sources. These Varangians were looking for ambers, furs, silver, and people to enslave. As the silver began to dry up, the Varangians also explored another of the main riverways, that of the Dnipro, making their way to the Black Sea and engaging with Constantinople and the Byzantine Empire. Before the Scandinavians took Kyiv and it became the capital of Rus, it was part of the territory of Khazaria, ruled from Itil on the lower Volga River. The Khazars were a particularly fascinating group of nomads who created a semi-nomadic state and whose elite converted to Judaism in approximately the eighth century.

Following these first interactions, our earliest Rusian source, the *Tale of Bygone Years*, tells how the various ninth-century groups of Slavs, Balts, and Finns 'invited' Riuryk and his two brothers (members of a group of Scandinavians known as Rus) to come and rule over the local populations. This so-called invitation is a much later creation by the royal family and their chroniclers, but it, and the very name of the mythical founder, Riuryk, have become embedded in our understanding of Rus and its place in Europe.

The creation of Kyivan Rus is often dated to 882, when a Rusian leader named Oleh (Helgi in Old Norse) took the city of Kyiv, uniting it with his base in the north of Novgorod. These became the two poles of Rus for more than two centuries. The importance of these cities is worth noting because Rus was a kingdom that would become the historical antecedent of Ukraine, as well as of Belarus and Russia; its lands also extended into modern Poland.

One of the most famous rulers of Kyivan Rus was Olha, later sainted in the Orthodox Church. She was the widow of Ihor, and regent for her minor son Sviatoslav in the mid-tenth century. Her rule was momentous for several reasons. First, all the Rusian rulers up to that point had had Scandinavian names – Oleh (Helgi), Ihor (Ingvar), and Olha (Helga) – but she and her husband gave their son a Slavic name (Sviatoslav), which was part of the ongoing acculturation of the Scandinavian ruling family with the local population that, in Kyiv, was largely Slavic. Second, Olha is well represented in the sources, as she travelled personally to Constantinople with a host of merchants and engaged in negotiations with the Byzantine emperor, receiving numerous gifts in return. Third, she was the first Christian ruler of Rus. It is typically thought that she converted to Christianity in Constantinople and took the name 'Helena' as a Christian name. Olha also

page 50
St Luke, Ostromir Gospel
(detail)
See Fig. 2, p. 58

attempted to bring a bishop and priests from the German Empire to convert her land. Though unsuccessful, this ploy marked her awareness of the place of Rus between two major empires and its position in Europe.

The Christianization of Rus as a whole would have to wait until the rule of Volodymyr, Olha's grandson, at the end of the tenth century. The *Tale of Bygone Years* records multiple conversion stories, and scholars have constructed yet another. Some of those that appear in the *Tale* include the 'calling of the faiths', in which representatives of Judaism, Islam, and Christianity (German and Byzantine) came to Rus to tell Volodymyr about their religions. This visit was the occasion for Volodymyr's *bon mot* that he could not convert to Islam because 'drink was the joy of the Rusians.' Another story involved the sending of emissaries to witness worship in various locations. The Rusians that were sent to Constantinople visited Hagia Sophia and declared that they 'knew not whether they were on Earth or in heaven'. The scholarly conversion story, however, begins with Volodymyr sending mercenaries to the Byzantine Emperor Basil II in exchange for a marriage agreement with Basil II's sister, Anna Porphyrogenita. The marriage of Anna to Volodymyr resulted in his Christianization, and when the two returned to Kyiv, the Christianization, or at least baptism, of the population of the city. Volodymyr ordered the citizens of Kyiv to gather at the Dnipro River for a mass baptism.

The rule of Yaroslav, Volodymyr's son, and his wife Ingigerd, a Swedish princess, is often considered to be the golden age of Rus. Bishops were sent throughout Rus, buildings and churches were constructed of stone, people began to be educated, monasteries were founded, and the royal family intermarried with European nobility. This golden age saw Rus stretching to become the largest territorial state in medieval Europe, from the Baltic in the north to the Black Sea in the south; from the frontiers with Poland and Hungary in the west to the Volga in the east. A German chronicler of the time even called Kyiv a 'rival to the sceptre of Constantinople'.

The twelfth century saw the rise of diverse regions within Rus, each vying to control Kyiv and to build their own power hubs. Novgorod in the north had been a centre of Rus since its foundation, and during this period its citizens began to actively choose their own rulers, participating in the wider politics of Rus in a new, more empowered way. In the east, Yurii Dolgorukii (Long-arm) and his son Andrei Bogoliubskii (God-loving) fashioned a new power centre in Vladimir–Suzdal between the Volga and Oka Rivers. In the southwest, Galicia and Volhynia were gaining authority through their persistent connections with the Hungarian and Polish ruling families, as well as ongoing ties to the Kyivan throne. These regions, existing together during this period in an uneasy dominion largely under Kyiv, would eventually fracture, and by the early thirteenth century, go their own ways.

In 1204, the Fourth Crusade sacked the city of Constantinople. This attack on an Orthodox Christian city by Latin Christian crusaders set the stage for a break between the churches, which had only been hinted at before this point. This split became more severe in 1222 when Pope Honorius III ordered the closing of Orthodox churches in Latin lands and the proselytization of Orthodox peoples to convert them to Latin Christianity. The final straw came with the declaration of crusades against Rus in the 1240s, leading to assaults on the Novgorod region by Latin Crusaders, which were defeated by Alexander Nevsky. The violence led to a stronger demarcation between Latin and Orthodox Christian identity that helped to create the idea of Orthodox Europe as separate from Latin Europe and contributed to the 'othering' of modern eastern Europe.

There were also attacks from the east during this time. The Mongols arrived to conquer the kingdom in the late 1230s and began to subjugate Rus, starting in the northeast with Riazan and eventually making their way to Kyiv by 1240, when they sacked the city on St Nicholas's day (6 December). The sack of Kyiv marks, for many, the end of Kyivan Rus. After this time, we see the various regions working independently of one another, with Kyiv exercising no dominion over any in particular. The Mongols governed Rus for much of the next two hundred years, though they were not the only power centre of the day. By the end of the thirteenth and the beginning of the fourteenth century, Lithuania began expanding into the former territories of Rus and absorbing them along the western Dvina River and into the Dnipro River valley. The influence of Lithuania, and later of the merged state of Poland–Lithuania, would shape the next stage of Rusian history. That phase, often identified as Ruthenia, witnessed the development of a Rusian territory inside the Polish–Lithuanian Commonwealth that has clearer links to the modern Ukrainian territory and identity that we know today.

(opposite)
St Sophia's Cathedral interior
Frescoes from 11th century
Kyiv

Marriage Connections

Kyivan Rus was deeply connected with the rest of medieval Europe. This was achieved in large part through a series of marriage arrangements between members of the ruling family of Rus and other European royals and elites. Following the first major dynastic marriage, between Volodymyr and Anna Porphyrogenita of Byzantium, several other unions blossomed. The children of Yaroslav and Ingigerd in particular married widely throughout Europe, to royalty in France, Hungary, Norway, and England, while later kings are known to have wed Polish, German, and Byzantine brides.

These marriages were part of a political process that saw individuals move throughout Europe, and introduced different languages, customs, and cultures. The Polish princess Gertrude, the wife of Yaroslav's son Iziaslav, brought with her to Rus a psalter that she most likely inherited from her German mother. In Rus, a Kyivan workshop helped to expand the psalter and add specific prayers for Gertrude, as well as illuminations accompanying the prayers. The image of *Christ Enthroned* (Fig. 1) shows Gertude's son Yaropolk and his wife Cunigunda receiving their crowns from Christ. The illuminations give us some of the only pictures of these Rusian individuals, while also demonstrating cultural blending: Byzantine-style dress and imagery are mixed with the Rusian preference for bold colours – gold and blue in particular, as seen in the cloisonné enamel-work of Rus – and Latin symbols for the Gospel writers. The same cultural synthesis can be seen in the image of St Luke from the Ostromir Gospel (Fig. 2, p. 58), and would not have happened without the interaction of these elites.

One interesting aspect of cultural transference is that of names. Yaroslav's daughter Anna's marriage to Henry I of France introduced the name Philip, that of her first-born son, into the Capetian royal line, where it became a mainstay. The marriage of Vsevolod (another of Yaroslav's sons that ruled Kyiv) to a Byzantine noblewoman gifted their son the sobriquet 'Monomakh' after the name of her clan – Monomachos. Monomakh himself married Gytha, the daughter of the last Anglo-Saxon king of England, Harold Godwinsson, and their son was known as Mstyslav in Rus, but as Harald in the Scandinavian sources where he appears regularly.

1
Christ Enthroned **from Codex 136**
c. 1078–86/87
Museo Nazionale Archeologico,
Cividale del Friuli, Italy

'Marriages were part of a political process that saw individuals move throughout Europe, and introduced different languages, customs, and cultures.'

t Luke, **Ostromir Gospel**
. 1056–57
National Library of Russia,
t Petersburg

late **spindle-whorls**
Examples of Ovruch spindle-
whorls from Drastar/Silistra

Finally, in the twelfth century, Mstyslav's daughter Ingiborg introduced the name Volodymyr into the Danish royal family, naming her son Valdemar. These tokens of cultural transference in the form of names help us to understand the important place of women in medieval European families and culture.

The movement of elites has often overshadowed that of other individuals. When a Russian princess went to another kingdom, as when Vsevolod's daughter Evpraksia travelled to the German Empire in the second half of the eleventh century, she took with her an entourage. The formulaic description of Evpraksia's impressive entourage includes camels, precious clothes and stones, and countless other riches. These could not all be carried by a single young woman, and the implication is that there were guards, ladies-in-waiting, servants of all stripes, and, due to her rank, a personal confessor. This escort created a small court, a centre of Russian culture in another kingdom. One of the few markers of non-elite women that have survived as artefacts are pink slate spindle-whorls. The pink slate came from a region of Rus, and yet these spindle-whorls have been found in many locations throughout medieval Europe. The spindle-whorl, used to spin thread, was commonly used by women in medieval Europe: we can imagine a woman carrying it with her wherever she went with her mistress, spreading Rusian material culture as she did so.

Arts and Crafts

Much of the material culture preserved from Kyivan Rus has been excavated throughout Rusian territory, in the modern countries of Ukraine, Russia, and Belarus in particular. The wealth of these finds highlights the diverse makers and objects that existed throughout the kingdom.

When the Scandinavian travellers first came down the eastern European river systems, one of the items they sought was amber. This precious material was used in jewelry throughout the medieval European world, and the Baltic coast became a prime source for amber exports. In Rus, as well as in Scandinavia, amber was frequently turned into beads and there are numerous preserved examples of both amber and glass beads found singly and as bracelets or necklaces. The beads in the necklaces shown may have been manufactured in Rus, where there were workshops for that purpose in a variety of locations, especially in Kyiv.

Russian craft centres in Novgorod and Kyiv produced jewelry and engraved work that stayed within the country as well as being exported to the rest of Europe. A cross with Slavonic writing on it, made in Novgorod, appeared in the twelfth

4 (*below*)
Beaded necklaces
10th–11th century
Cemetery near Brovarky,
Poltava oblast
National Museum of the
History of Ukraine, Kyiv

5 (*opposite, right*)
Bulgarian-style bracelet
14th century
Vasylytsia, Cherkasy oblast
National Museum of the
History of Ukraine, Kyiv

6 (*opposite, left*)
Kolti
11th–12th century
Cloisonné enamel, gold
National Museum of the
History of Ukraine, Kyiv

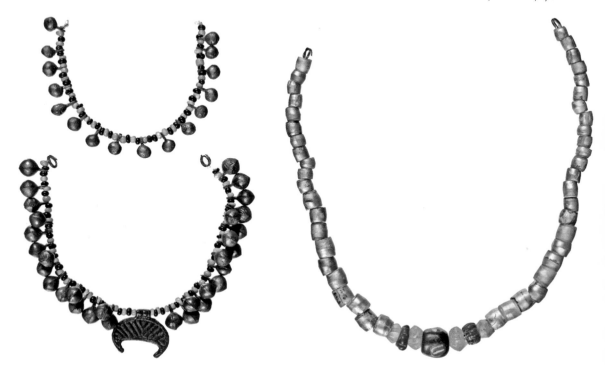

century in Hildesheim in the German Empire, for instance. Unfortunately, much of the metalwork made in Rus or that was imported into Rus was most likely melted down over the years for currency, though excavations are still turning up materials throughout the former Rus lands, such as the silver bracelet in a Bulgarian style from the fourteenth century (Fig. 5).

One of the most distinctive Rusian ornaments, often found in museum collections, are kolti. These pendants are meant to hang from a headdress, usually on either side of the face. They have a hollow centre into which perfume-soaked cloth was inserted, presumably so that sweet smells would waft toward the wearer. While typically assumed to be a marker of female dress, there are images of men wearing kolti as well, for instance, in Serbia later in the medieval period. Rusian temple pendants are typically made of gold with decoration in cloisonné enamel – a classic choice that emphasized the bright colours that we also see in manuscript illumination. The enamel designs on the pendants typically have geometric patterns on the back, while the front may show sirens, a tree of life, or various other decorations.

Archaeological excavations have unearthed not just these objects, but also the means of their creation, including numerous stone moulds used for making pendants, earrings, crosses, and much more. The preservation of so many moulds indicates that there was a flourishing trade in these goods, as well as numerous production centres in and around Kyiv. Given the remaining trace metals, we can also tell that the items were not always made of gold, but also of less precious alternatives, the final products of which have not been preserved. It is important to note that artistic culture stretched beyond the elite, and while the surviving examples may be of high-quality gold and fine niello or cloisonné work, the majority of craft objects were probably made for the regular inhabitants of Kyiv.

A Connected World

Extensive trade networks linked Kyivan Rus firmly with the rest of western Eurasia. The earliest Scandinavian explorers coming down the eastern European river systems found silver dirhams – coins originating from the Abbasid Caliphate, an Islamic polity with its capital in Baghdad. Silver dirhams were a popular currency due to their standardization: they were used not only in the Middle East, but also around the Caspian Sea and traded up the Volga River, which is where the Varangians first took notice of them. They took those coins back home to Scandinavia, and set up outposts in what would become Rus to gather further coins, as well as furs, amber, and enslaved people. Over time, imitation dirhams (Fig. 7) were created, on which the Arabic script is simply gibberish that imitates Arabic. Modelling one's own coinage on such an impressive currency was a way to add value and to make the coin as credible as an original dirham. The imitation of Arabic script also lends strength to the idea that in this period the image of writing was more powerful than the content of the writing itself, suggesting that, in a sense, literacy was considered 'magical'.

The Khazars were a semi-nomadic Turkic people that ruled Kyiv before the Scandinavians. Itil, capital of Khazaria until the tenth century, was home to Muslims, Christians, Jews, and pagans, and was reputed to have judges for each group to help maintain law and order. The Kyivan Letter, found in the Cairo Genizah (the largest collection of medieval Jewish and Fatimid documents, discovered in Ben Ezra Synagogue in Cairo, Egpyt), is famous because it includes a marking, indicating that the letter had been read by local Khazar officials. The use of Hebrew for government activity has helped advance our understanding of the Khazar elite's conversion to Judaism and the extent that the religion (and the language) formed part of the government apparatus.

Kyiv, as the capital of Rus, maintained ties over a broad area. Trade was conducted via the various gates of the city. The Golden Gate (its name appropriated from its Constantinopolitan counterpart) led to the south, and it can be understood

7
Imitation dirham
9th–10th century
Silver
Sumy oblast

3
Kyivan Letter (detail)
10th century
Cambridge University Library

(*overleaf*)
**Golden Gate
(Zoloti Vorota)**
11th century; rebuilt 1982
Kyiv

as a marker of trade with the Byzantine Empire. The gate, as reconstructed from archaeological evidence, is massive, and would have been an imposing fixture for anyone approaching the city. Atop the gate was a fully functioning church that served the local community, but which was also part of the sanctification of the defences of Kyiv from invaders. Of course, much of that trade also took place via the Dnipro River and thus came into and out of the upper city of Kyiv through the Podol Gate. Located on the river's banks, the Podol was the marketplace and craft centre. The Dnipro not only handled trade downstream to the Black Sea and Byzantium, but also goods that came from upstream. Rus had robust connections with Scandinavia, and, alongside trade, people travelled south from Novgorod, carrying their boats overland between rivers to reach the upper Dnipro before coming down to Kyiv itself. The Jewish Gate of the city faced southwest and trade through there ran to Hungary and into Europe. There is a great deal of evidence for Jewish travellers and traders going from Central Europe to Rus and beyond to Central Asia, from the time of the earliest foundation of Rus until the twelfth century. The Polish Gate of the city was directed to the southeast; its name indicates the importance for Rus of trade with Poland. All of this presents a picture of Kyiv as situated within a web of trading relationships stretching north to south, which are often emphasized, as well as from east to west, which are not. It was an enormously well-connected centre in western Eurasia.

Military Engagements

Being part of an interconnected world meant that it was common for Rus to experience conflict with its neighbours, as well as within its own boundaries. This is not to say that Rus was prone to violence; rather, violence was endemic to medieval life and often occurred on a small scale, with belligerents numbering only in the hundreds and with routes to a settlement on all sides.

The most common adversaries of the period were nomadic peoples from the steppe. These nomads included the Khazars, the Pechenegs, the Polovtsy, and eventually the Mongols. In the late tenth century, Sviatoslav defeated the Khazars and may have unintentionally opened the steppe to new arrivals such as the Pechenegs, who moved to the region soon afterward, and repeatedly threatened Kyiv. Volodymyr, son of Sviatoslav, built a series of towns south of Kyiv to buttress the city's defences. At the same time, he erected the first fortification at what would later become the Khotyn Fortress. Originally, this was a simple motte-and-bailey construction of wood and dirt, but by the thirteenth century it had been rebuilt in stone as a key part of the defences of Halych. Volodymyr (Sviatoslav's son and Olha's grandson), also erected the Snake Ramparts, a series of earthen walls along rivers south of Kyiv, to delay nomadic invasions and to help defenders. These massive fortifications took a great deal of time and manpower and were a testament to the organizational impetus of Volodymyr. Despite the presence of the Snake Ramparts, however, nomad incursions continued throughout the period, with notable victories such as Yaroslav's defeat of the Pechenegs in 1036. The Rusians were not the only ones to suffer such attacks: the Palanok Castle in western Ukraine was initially erected as a Hungarian border fort to protect against these same nomadic raiders, and was only much later absorbed into Ukrainian territory.

10
Khotyn Fortress
11th century
Chernivtsi oblast

'These massive fortifications took a great deal of time and manpower and were a testament to the organizational impetus of Volodymyr.'

Internal strife also occurred, such as when Yaroslav, then ruling in Novgorod, refused to pay tribute to his father Volodymyr in Kyiv. Volodymyr ordered the roads to be repaired for war. This brief event – and it is little more than that, as Volodymyr died before the campaign began – provides fascinating information about roads and the requirements of their upkeep in Rus. Winter campaigns would also have been carried out in Rus, when frozen rivers could be used as highways to travel more easily than in the muddy autumn or spring weather. One of the most notable internal conflicts occurred in the late eleventh century when a Rusian prince, Vasylko Rostyslavych, was blinded at the instigation of his political opponents. Such a punishment, common in Byzantium for usurpers, was a bridge too far for

most of the Rusian elite, who condemned the act and put a limit on what rulers could and could not do to their foes in future.

Another power struggle, showing the reach of Rusian ties, occurred in 1149. That year, Yurii Dolgorukii took Kyiv from his nephew, Iziaslav Mstyslavych. In an attempt to regain his city, Iziaslav called on a host of relations. The Hungarian king could not come himself, but sent several thousand cavalry. Bolesław IV and his brother Heinrich came with their soldiers from Poland, and Vladislav II from Bohemia came with his own troops. Though no military engagement resulted, this event was significant because most of east-central Europe was represented in one place, all contesting the ownership of Kyiv.

The attacks by the Mongols and the crusaders in the thirteenth century brought Rusian warriors into contact with forces from both east and west. The metal helmet shown here is the typical type worn by a Rusian warrior. It is a conical metal cap that would protect the wearer in case of a direct hit on the head by deflecting the blow to the sides. This type of helmet has also been found in much more highly decorated versions engraved with images of saints, such as St George, from later years. The engagements with both the Mongols and the crusaders helped to define the position of Rus going forward, but those attacks were also indicative of Rus being situated in a larger medieval world.

12
Helmet
13th century
Height 181 mm; diameter
244 × 210 mm
Found at the Church
of the Tithes, Kyiv
National Museum of the
History of Ukraine, Kyiv

Religious Ties

When Olha, Ihor's wife and ruler of Kyivan Rus, converted to Christianity (see p. 52), she had a priest in her entourage – evidence that the religion was already present in Rus. Whether Olha converted in Byzantium or elsewhere (a question that remains contested), she was certainly a Christian at the time of her death. Her grandson Volodymyr's conversion to Christianity took place in the city of Kherson, carried out by the local priests, after he captured the city from the Byzantines. The subsequent baptism of the people of Kyiv – at his instigation – was performed by priests brought back from Kherson, as well as the priests that had travelled with his wife, Anna Porphyrogenita, from Constantinople. In fact, soon after Volodymyr's conversion, it is thought that the pope in Rome sent relics of St Clement to Volodymyr to celebrate the event. All of this informs us that, despite the predominant perception that Rus converted 'with Byzantium' and thus tied itself to Byzantium in perpetuity, that was not quite the case. Both Olha and Volodymyr were aware of their position between two empires and of the power of conversion, and they worked hard to maintain a delicate balance.

13
***St George and Scenes
from His Life***
12th century
Wood with tempera over
gesso and traces of gilding
National Art Museum
of Ukraine, Kyiv

The majority of preserved artistic works from Rus clearly demonstrate Byzantine influence on the Church. Icons are particularly representative of Byzantine style, and there is a prevalence of St George icons in Rus because the ruling family, following the lead of the Byzantine emperors, honoured a series of warrior saints. The icon of *St George and Scenes from His Life* (Fig. 13, p. 71) shows St George standing, which is not his typical pose; in most icons he is astride his horse and slaying a dragon. Here, however, he is surrounded by several smaller images that illustrate scenes from his life, hence the title of the work. This type of icon would have helped to show the mainly pre-literate audience the glory of the Christian saints and to illustrate stories from the saints' lives that might be told by priests, as well as during church services.

The Rusian royal family, following the lead of many other ruling dynasties throughout Europe, also created their own saints. In Rus, these were the brothers Borys and Hlib, the sons of Volodymyr. To prevent a potential threat to his rule, another of Volodymyr's sons, Sviatopolk 'the Accursed', had them killed after he succeeded to the throne of Kyiv in 1015. The two responded to the news of their impending death sentences with quiet acceptance and thus achieved sainthood as 'passion-sufferers' in the image of Jesus Christ. They were quickly canonized in Rus and became familiar figures on icons displayed throughout the realm, as well as important dedicatees of churches, particularly in the Chernihiv area.

Byzantine style in Rus extended to architecture, which we can see in the most famous church in Kyiv, St Sophia's. This church, named after the Hagia Sophia in Constantinople (both names mean 'holy wisdom'), retains its Byzantine looks to this day – even after it was rebuilt during the Ukrainian Baroque period of the seventeenth and eighteenth centuries (see pp. 110–33). The original church was more understated but still quite beautiful, with numerous domes, though no cupolas as such, and a large interior space that was designed to evoke the sense that Hagia Sophia gave visitors, of an enormous interior dedicated to God (see p. 54). The original church design is commemorated on the Ukrainian two-hryvnia banknote. The modelling of Byzantine styles in Rus was a way to appropriate some of the grandeur of the greatest empire in western Eurasia for the newly Christianized kingdom.

14 (*opposite*)
Borys and Hlib
Mid-14th century
Tempera on wood
Height 142.5 cm; width 94.3 cm
Kyiv Picture Gallery

15 (*below*)
St Sophia's Cathedral, Kyiv
Byzantine model illustrated on two-hryvnia banknote

16 (*overleaf*)
St Sophia's Cathedral, Kyiv
Present-day aerial view

Many different forms of artistic wood carving are represented across Ukraine, with great regional variation. Wooden products – revealing local features, styles, shapes, and finishes – range from carved crosses, plates and bowls, utensils, and chests to wooden figurines.

Mother's Kiss
V. I. Svyd (1912–89)
1959
Uzhhorod, Zakarpattia oblast
Carved wood

Archangel Michael
18th century
Sytniaki, Kyiv oblast
Carved and painted wood

Bandurist
P. P. Verna (1876–1966)
1912
Boryspil, Kyiv oblast
Carved and painted wood

In the late nineteenth and early twentieth centuries, folk Christianity flourished in Ukraine, especially in rural regions. Infusing folk art with Christian imagery, a number of these Ukrainian wooden figurines are religious in nature. See page 242.

Saviour
18th century
Middle Dnipro, Poltava oblast
Carved and painted wood

Mother of God (*left*)
Early 20th century
Carved and painted wood

John (*right*)
Early 20th century
Carved and painted wood

Saviour
Volodymyr Asenovich Saliuk
(1870–1945)
Late 19th century
Podillia
Carved and painted wood

THE GRAND DUCHY
OF LITHUANIA

14th to 16th centuries

Diana Klochko

A fter the disintegration of Kyivan Rus, following devastating Mongol invasions in the 1230s and early 1240s, the Grand Duchy of Lithuania emerged in the thirteenth century as an alliance of Lithuanian and Ukrainian princes. One of the first goals of this newly formed Duchy was to gain independence from the Golden Horde, the Mongol khanate whose reach stretched across large swathes of eastern Europe. The Duchy defeated the Golden Horde in the Battle of Blue Waters in 1362, and the Horde lost its right to collect tribute on the lands between the Baltic and the Black Sea. The Grand Duchy of Lithuania then became one of the largest states in contemporary Europe, dominated by the linguistic, cultural, and sociopolitical traditions of Kyivan Rus. In fact, the Galician–Volhynian Chronicle, a historical record detailing events of the thirteenth century, states that the union of the Duchy was a sign that the Lithuanian princes were aligned with Kyivan culture. Reflecting this multiplicity of cultures, Ukrainian art from the fourteenth to the sixteenth century portrayed a variety of different individuals and communities, layered in a palimpsest of the old and new.

The Duchy's rule preserved existing principalities and lands as units of administration, and carried on the existing system of governance, merely replacing the preceding Riuryk dynasty with new rulers, the Gediminids. Laws of the land were based on Ruska Pravda, the legal code of Kyivan Rus, and the arrangements created in Kyivan Rus continued to function in both the military sphere and in the administration of tax collection. The precursor of parliament – the Council of Lords, an assembly of noble family representatives – was established in the following century to act as a check on the power of the Grand Dukes. Within the council, Ruthenian magnates who owned vast lands and benefited from abundant assets (which allowed them to recruit, employ, and lead military units) enjoyed the greatest influence. For instance, at the Battle of Orsha in 1514, the army of Kostiantyn Ostrozkyi, a Ruthenian prince and magnate of the Duchy, routed the combined forces of the Muscovite–German alliance. The news of this victory was publicized in pamphlets printed in German and Latin. Ostrozkyi was hailed as a hero in Warsaw and Vilnius, where he founded two churches in honour of his success, sponsored schools, and later financed the Ostroh Bible, the first complete printed bible published in Church Slavonic (see Fig. 12, p. 100).

The Orthodox Church also retained its influence on the cultural and social development of the state, specifically through the confraternities (brotherhoods) it supported. The oldest of these – the Lviv Dormition Brotherhood (founded in 1439) and the Vilnius Kushnirski Brotherhood (founded in 1458) – helped set up an electoral system, and provided aid to churches, hospitals, and schools. Confraternity schools were lay institutions; nonetheless, their rhetoric of 'defending the faith of our fathers' against Catholicism and Protestantism eventually evolved into a public

page 78
Virgin Hodegetria
of Volhynia (detail)
See Fig. 7, p. 93

polemic disseminated in pamphlets and tracts that argued in favour of reforming the Orthodox Church, and criticized the conservatism of its leadership. The emergence of reformist movements, especially those inspired by the Czech philosopher and reformist Jan Hus, along with the increased economic status of city dwellers who benefited from organizing into guilds under Magdeburg Law (a legal code giving autonomy to individual towns, brought to Ukraine by colonists originating in what is now Germany), were reflected as new trends in the visual culture of the time. 'Orthodox' became synonymous with 'ancient', while being 'current' required a different style of personal presentation. This was embodied in urban architecture through the construction of European-style townhouses and palaces. In other arts, the same trend prompted a fashion for so-called Sarmatian portraiture (see p. 101) and a new interest in theatre. Urban planners, meanwhile, sought to amend the existing defence systems of most Grand Duchy cities – dominated by a keep with a fortress and walls punctuated by guard towers – with secular public spaces, designed by architects who espoused the ideals of 'a perfect city', such as Petro Italiets (a citizen of Lviv, originally from Lugano) or Vincenzo Scamozzi. Before the end of the sixteenth century, eight architects born in Italian-speaking Swiss cantons, as well as in Rome and Venice, became citizens of Lviv.

The first books in early forms of the Ukrainian language were printed in the late fifteenth century in Kraków and Prague. With time, confraternities established their own print shops to supply grammar books and first readers to their schools. These textbooks were written and translated by local urban intellectuals. Łukasz from Nowe Miasto, a scholar of Liberal Arts at Kraków University, published the first textbook on letter writing in 1522. The first grammar of Church Slavonic, compiled in Ostroh, was published in Vilnius, in 1586. By the early sixteenth century, there were nearly eighty universities in Europe, and almost all of them had students or representatives from the Grand Duchy (at Kraków University, for example, there were thirteen professors from the so-called Ruthenian lands). When they returned home, they took up government service, or became judges or military experts at various levels – as was documented in Cossack registries of the sixteenth century.

The Cossacks were a semi-nomadic group from the steppes. In the sixteenth century, they were a professional military class, offering armed services (for example, protecting the Duchy against Tatar raids) in exchange for rights such as self-governance. Their semi-autonomous state was called the Zaporizhian Sich. The Cossacks had a pragmatic approach to acquiring knowledge. Realizing that intelligence gathering, diplomacy, and the art of war would be impossible without the command of foreign languages, the Cossack leadership identified talented young people early, and benefactors, too, if needed, and even allocated stipends from the funds of the Zaporizhian Sich to enable the students to attend universities.

Armenian Cathedral, Lviv (interior)
See page 90

As the practices of Magdeburg Law spread to a greater number of cities, giving them increased political autonomy, efforts in urban planning became more concerted. Older cities such as Kyiv, Volodymyr, Chernihiv, and Novhorod-Siverskyi, however, retained their ancient layouts, determined by their physical terrain and dominated by churches. Large monasteries became fortress-like, with walls and towers. These institutions supported scriptoria and icon-painting workshops, which followed not so much ideological dictates as emerging aesthetic models. Especially after the fall of Constantinople in 1453, when examples of the city's icon-painting traditions were no longer produced, the few surviving icons from the eleventh to thirteenth century came to be regarded as 'miracle-working'. These pieces, darkened with age, were copied and protected with cloth covers.

Ukrainian painting developed in various forms: frescoes, icons, book miniatures, and secular portraits. Many of the frescoes mentioned in various chronicles have not survived, though a few are preserved in Poland, such as those in the Holy Trinity Chapel in Lublin and the Chapel of the Holy Cross in Kraków's Wawel Castle. Icon painting mainly adhered to canonical types, especially in the portrayal of the Holy Mother of God and of saints, though during this period new compositions and character types were added, including members of different religious communities, ethnicities, and social classes – for example, in multi-figure paintings of the Last Judgment or the Passion of Christ. The dimensions of most icons preserved from this period suggest that they were not intended for private residences, but were destined for churches that used a traditional three-tier altar partition. In some cases, perhaps in wealthier churches, an iconostasis was installed with several tiers of icons, but even this did not form a screen that entirely obscured the view of the altar (as it does in the Russian Orthodox tradition, which hides the sacrament from the faithful).

The nobility and princes of the Grand Duchy funded, and invited foreign artists to work on, churches, chapels, and private residences. Travelling merchants brought with them collections of portraits painted by Italian and German masters. For instance, the Radziwiłł Palace (Olyka Castle) had a portrait hall with paintings that included works by the German Renaissance painter Lucas Cranach the Elder. Local painters created a distinctive genre of portraiture, rooted in the notion that the nobles and Cossacks shared common ancestors known as ancient Sarmatians. These artists borrowed elements of Renaissance portraiture and Mannerist accoutrements such as coats of arms and inscriptions to create images that emphasized the sitter's status and membership in a specific community, rather than their inner life, intellectual interests, or physical beauty. The painting technique in these portraits is generally uniform, with great attention paid to the detailing of luxurious clothing. Gestures were codified and facial expressions fixed. These portraits, because of their predilection for the decorative, became akin to family crests. A rare example of a sculptural Sarmatian-style portrait is the marble tomb of Prince Kostiantyn Ostrozkyi, in the early Italian Renaissance style. The prince, who funded the creation of the Ostroh Bible (Fig. 12, p. 100), commissioned the tomb and it was installed in 1579 in the Holy Dormition Cathedral of Kyiv-Pecherska Lavra. The significance of Kyivan heritage, as preserved and embodied by monasticism, remained an important factor in the spiritual life of even the land's most progressive personalities.

The Era of Castle-Building

Following the Mongol invasions, led out of Asia by Batu Khan in the late 1230s and early 1240s, people of the Ukrainian lands spent nearly half a century rebuilding their economic and artistic lives. Beginning in the early fourteenth century, local princes invested in building fortresses to house garrisons and their administrative offices in case of sudden hostilities between neighbours, or even members of the same family. Often, such fortifications included a keep, which served as the feudal lord's residence, housing his court and service staff. To erect these fortresses, the builders reused materials from the ruins of earlier fortifications, sometimes dating back to pre-Christian times, as was the case with the Genoese Fortress in Sudak, Crimea, and the Tustan Fortress in the Carpathians. Defences were situated to take maximum advantage of the existing topography and access to rivers, since the waterways remained reliable transportation routes year-round. The Dnister, the Dnipro, and the Danube Rivers, with their many tributaries, represented an internal trade-route network widely used to move – and therefore to control – various goods, troops, and military equipment.

Fortress builders implemented the latest technologies learned in western European cities to create new defensive cityscapes in Ukraine. The Palanok Castle in Mukachevo (Transcarpathia), Akkerman Fortress in Bilhorod-Dnistrovskyi (Odesa oblast), the Khotyn Fortress on the Dnister (Chernivtsi oblast), and the High Castle (*Vysokyi Zamok* in Ukrainian) in Lviv all share such features as tall defensive walls with embrasures, moats, and drawbridges. Even villages often featured fortified churches as, for instance, in the village of Sutkivtsi in Khmelnytskyi oblast. Not all fortresses have survived to the present day in their original form, but we can extrapolate their scale and aesthetics from those that have been preserved.

The first mention of Lutsk Castle (also known as Liubart's Castle) dates to 1085, but the building of the higher keep was begun under the reign of Prince Liubart in the 1350s. Through the ages, the number and height of the castle's towers, roofed with wood shingle, has varied. The masonry of the gate tower shows traces of multiple additions. The castle served as the prince's residence, and after the Union of Lublin (an agreement with the Kingdom of Poland that formed the Polish–

1
Lutsk Castle (Liubart's Castle)
Mid-14th century
Lutsk, Volyn oblast

'The local community cherished the sense of belonging to a large European family for a long time, with details of the extraordinary summit told and retold for years.'

Lithuanian Commonwealth in 1569), it became the seat of the royal government in the Volhynian Voivodeship (administrative region) from 1569 to 1795. A prestigious residential neighbourhood then formed around the castle's walls, filled with rich city dwellers and government and church officials.

In 1429, the palace of the higher keep hosted a summit of European monarchs, a high-level diplomatic meeting that also included three Tatar Khans. The Grand Duke Vytautas convened fellow European rulers, as well as envoys from Constantinople and Papal representatives, to discuss the threat posed by the Ottoman Empire, the problem of Jan Hus's religious reform movement, and his own coronation. The occasion brought nearly fifteen thousand people to Lutsk, several times the city's regular population. Guests were supplied with hundreds of barrels of wine and beer and wild boar, moose, bison, and wild-sheep meat, in addition to numerous gold and silver utensils. The hosts put up a jousting ground and made arrangements for royal hunts. The local community cherished the sense of belonging to a large European family for a long time, with details of the extraordinary summit told and retold for years. A depiction of the Lutsk Castle gate tower now features on the 200-hryvnia banknote.

To the south of Volhynia, the various rulers of Podillia – a land where militancy often outweighed any impulse to unify – were similarly ambitious. In the fourteenth century, the city of Kamianets became the capital of an independent Podillia principality, and its ruling duumvirate, the brothers Kostiantyn and Fedir Koriatovych, began the construction of their fortress here in 1374. At about the same time, the city received Magdeburg rights and soon became a large trade hub. The island on which the Kamianets-Podilskyi Fortress is located is encircled by a canyon along which the River Smotrych flows – a stunning sight. The castle is connected to the city proper by a bridge to a narrow promontory. Built to withstand firearms and artillery, the towers, upper rooms, and supports of the castle walls are made entirely of stone. The fortress, with its diamond-shaped plan, tall walls and eleven towers, was considered impregnable. Each tower has a proper name and features coats of arms and inscriptions in Latin, made at different dates. One of these, a rather pessimistic VERVS AMICVS EST RARIOR FENICE ('A true friend is rarer than a phoenix'), captures the spirit of the bellicose era.

A 1960 archaeological excavation under the building that connected the Black tower with the Pope's tower revealed a cannon-maker's room, stocked with enormous stone cannonballs. The dig also found the Koriatovych burial chamber, eight metres deep, carved into the bedrock of the castle. The fortress well, which was still in use as late as the nineteenth century, is even deeper: it took several men to operate its wheels, located on two different levels. The city lived its own life outside the fortress walls, but its residents were no doubt well aware of how to navigate

2
Kamianets-Podilskyi Fortress
14th century
Kamianets-Podilskyi,
Khmelnytskyi oblast

the inside of it should an enemy threaten the city. Not all fortifications had defence plans as clear and elaborate as those of Kamianets, and few could benefit from such extraordinary topography. Most castles of this period are preserved in the region of Galicia, where there are over thirty, in various conditions, in the Ternopil oblast alone.

One of the oldest castles in Ukraine stands on a flat hill in the small town of Olesko (Lviv oblast). First mentioned in 1327, the castle is described as having a spacious courtyard surrounded by a stone wall, and a single entrance gate protected by a tower. These walls are still preserved in the lower levels of the castle, where original rooms were converted to storage spaces after two new levels accommodating residential quarters were built between the sixteenth and eighteenth centuries. Olesko Castle was located on the border between Galicia and Volhynia – a great political advantage for its holders – and was therefore contested for centuries by noble families of Lithuania and Poland. The future Hetman (head of state) of Ukraine Bohdan Khmelnytskyi spent his childhood at Olesko, while Jan III Sobieski, the King of Poland, called 'the saviour of Europe' after his victory over the Ottomans at Vienna in 1683, was born here. The castle still holds the table and the bed that were, according to local lore, the king's favourites whenever he visited the castle with his beloved queen consort, the French-born Marie Casimire Louise de La Grange d'Arquien. In the second half of the twentieth century, the castle was declared a protected museum. Its renovated interiors, in several historical styles, now feature period marble mantels, heraldic reliefs, and a collection of art from the fourteenth to the eighteenth century.

(overleaf)
Olesko Castle
14th century
Olesko, Lviv oblast

Religious Art and Architecture of Different Nations

The Grand Duchy government was relatively tolerant toward the various faiths and religious communities: Orthodox Christians and Catholics held equal rights; Muslim Tatars were allowed to settle (although only in certain places); and Jews had a degree of religious autonomy following a charter in 1388 (though they were exiled from Lithuania for eight years in 1495, and severely persecuted at other times). These various groups had free choice of style and materials for their churches and other religious buildings.

The Armenian Cathedral of Lviv was built in the 1360s with funding from Kaffa-based merchants. The commissioners chose an Italian architect from Genoa named Dorchi (also known as Doring) to supervise local Armenian craftspeople in Lviv. The structure and proportions of the building attest to Doring's talent for finding a harmonious combination of Italian, Byzantine, and Armenian architectural traditions. After a fire in 1381, renovation work that lasted until 1437 added Renaissance elements to the cathedral. For centuries, members of the Armenian community were buried under the floor of the church and the pavement of its courtyard. The church's interior contained frescoes that date back to the fifteenth century – these were discovered by a restoration team in 1925. Later, Jan Henryk de Rosen's frescoes (painted from 1926 to 1929) added an Art Deco aesthetic to the Byzantine–Armenian synthesis apparent in this unique building.

4
Armenian Cathedral
1363
Lviv

The book-making legacy of this era also confirms that the Grand Duchy rulers held their Byzantine heritage in high regard. Kyiv became a part of the Grand Duchy in 1394, and in 1397 the scriptoria that was likely adjacent to St Sophia's Cathedral wrote, illuminated, and bound one of the most magnificent books of eastern Europe in the Middle Ages, the *Kyiv Psalter*. The book was made of 230 vellum sheets, and includes 300 miniatures painted with powdered precious stones and gold, among other pigments. The Grand Duke Vytautas provided most of the funding for the book, as evidenced by the dedication, which also states that the volume was made in Kyiv. It is likely that such a prized liturgical object was meant to play a role in Vytautas's plan for unifying the realm. St Sophia's was the location of the main seat of the Metropolitan Bishop of Kyiv and All Rus until the Great Schism of 1054. Publishing the new translation of the Psalter in 1397, written by the Metropolitan bishop Kyprian, would have strengthened the unity of the Orthodox Church, as well

as providing the foundation for uniting several princedoms with predominantly Orthodox populations. This treasure of Kyiv's visual culture, adorned with exceptionally well-executed miniatures, is currently 'in exile'. For a long time, the volume was kept in Vilnius. During the Polish uprising of 1864, it was requisitioned by the Russian Empire. There, it was kept in the Sheremetev family's Fountain House in St Petersburg until 1932, when it was made state property of the USSR following a fire.

Crimea's Tatar population and Muslim heritage similarly exemplifies cultural refinements during the period. The Crimean Khanate won its independence from the Golden Horde under the leadership of Hacı I Giray, whose family were descendants of Genghis Khan. In 1532, Sahib I Giray, Khan of Crimea, funded the building of one of the peninsula's largest mosques as part of his palace in Bakhchysarai (Fig. 6). The arcade on the ground floor, combined with majolica inserts in the windows and the four-sided roof covered in red tiles, lends the building its airy, festive appearance. The interior of the large hall with its tall columns is lit through stained-glass windows. A spiral staircase leads to the broad balcony. The building has a separate entrance into the Khan's dedicated room, richly decorated with majolica tiles and stained glass. In 2017, the occupying government of the Russian Federation began restoration work that has significantly damaged the mosque. Now lost are the authentic beam structure under the mosque's roof, many stained-glass windows, and the four-sided roof itself. The original spoon-shaped artisanal roof tiles ('tatarka') have also been replaced with modern, industrially produced versions.

6
Great Khan Mosque
1532
Bakhchysarai, Crimea

Byzantine Traditions in Christian Art

The multi-confessional environment and relative religious tolerance enshrined in the Grand Duchy's laws supported shifts in artistic attitudes toward Byzantine traditions in Orthodox art. This transformation enabled the emergence of regional, non-metropolitan schools of painting.

The icon known as the *Virgin Hodegetria of Volhynia* is exceptional among works of sacred painting created in the Volhynia region of northwestern Ukraine in the fourteenth century. The colour scheme is limited, and the image itself combines a strong graphic presence and a tragic mood, with considered embellishment. The edge of the Virgin's cloak is decorated with ribbons and tassels, and the infant Jesus wears an embroidered shirt, probably representative of local Volhynian garments. The Virgin gazes at the viewer with understanding, but also reproachfully. Jesus is

7
Virgin Hodegetria of Volhynia
Late 14th century
85 × 48 cm
National Art Museum of Ukraine,
Kyiv

portrayed as a mature, stern, divine person who is well aware of his future suffering for the sins of mankind. The addition of dark shadows under their eyes indicates the painter's desire to break away from the strict linear portrayal of the subjects. Having made the choice to portray the Virgin in three-quarter view, the painter also gave her eyes different sizes, in an attempt, evidently, to show perspective.

In the fifteenth century, the emergence of local workshops in cities and within large monasteries gradually displaced the preference for 'travelling' icons brought from Constantinople. Local artists were permitted significant deviation from the canon and experimented with colours, adding details seen in works by Catholic painters, and with more complex composition. The tastes of their patrons, often wealthy merchants who personally discussed the details they wanted to see in the commissioned work, prompted the emergence of imagery that was earlier considered foreign. For instance, icons representing St George first appeared during the rule of Yaroslav the Wise, who venerated St George as his heavenly patron. Beginning in the fourteenth century, however, painters in the princedoms exposed to the European Gothic style started to portray St George as a knight defeating a dragon and rescuing a princess.

The icon of *St George the Dragon-Slayer*, from the latter half of the fifteenth century, shows how far an artist could push the boundaries of tradition with local inflection. The viewer recognizes the saint by his red cloak, which unfurls in stiff folds behind the warrior's back, while the rest of his dress conforms in every detail to the Byzantine standard. The surprise comes once we find a dragon that deviates dramatically from its typical depiction as a three-tailed serpent. Next to the sharp-toothed maw of the wingless creature is the small figure of a girl wearing a crown: the frightened victim, on her knees outside a large castle. The princess's parents, the king and queen, watch from the windows with their heads propped on their hands; their expressions are as engaged as those of the armoured guards and many service-people who are present at the scene. No longer an image of the metaphysical struggle between good and evil in which an angel's hand guides the saint's lance, this is much more an illustration of a knightly joust outside the city's gates. The icon presented its owners with an opportunity to admire the many-towered, elaborate city-castle whose flags reach the sky. Such a mixture of styles, with European elements woven into the Byzantine sacred art canon, represents one of the dominant trends of the period.

Monumental portrayals of the Passion of Christ, composed of multiple boards, also emerged in the fifteenth century. Ancient Ukrainian tradition placed frescoes of these scenes on the walls of the nave. Whenever a church could not afford such

8
St George the Dragon-Slayer
Latter half of 15th century
114 × 79 cm
National Art Museum of Ukraine, Kyiv

'The icon of *St George the Dragon-Slayer*, which dates to the latter half of the fifteenth century, shows how far an artist could push the boundaries of tradition with local inflection.'

9
Panels showing Holy Passion
Late 16th century
Tempera on gesso-grounded
wood panels
Central board 202 × 64 cm
Left and right boards 202 × 25 cm
National Art Museum of Ukraine,
Kyiv

a painting, it would replace it with an icon. It is reasonable to assume that the composition boards were influenced by the painters' experience of mystery plays, which they no doubt witnessed at Catholic churches during Holy Week, and which would have been full of details they could later recreate in their paintings. For instance, panels showing the Holy Passion from Galicia (Fig. 9) are composed of three boards, each over two metres tall. They depict separate episodes, put together much like a cartoon strip, with expansive inscriptions on each picture. These texts come from the sermons of the local priest who commissioned the icon and contain his interpretations of the biblical text. Priests at the time were fluent in both Greek and Latin, and the congregations, even in rural churches, could easily read Old Ukrainian.

Adopting European Styles

In many regions where patrons had the economic means to invite foreign groups of artists, local artists regularly came into contact with colleagues who worked outside of the Byzantine canon. The Horianska Rotunda of St Anna's Church is located in Horiany, a district of today's city of Uzhhorod. Experts from several countries have confirmed that the building was erected in the Romanesque style and that the frescoes inside (Fig. 10) can be attributed to a team of painters who were the Italian artist Giotto's students and worked in the fourteenth and fifteenth centuries. A branch of the noble family of Drugeth also owned an estate in Horiany. Count Derd Drugeth, the Lord of Uzhhorod, favoured Italian painting, so it is possible he invited a group of itinerant painters to accompany him when he moved from Naples in 1354.

10
Fresco in Horianska Rotunda, St Anna's Church
14th–15th century
Uzhhorod, Zakarpattia oblast

'Since the declaration of Ukraine's independence in 1991, [the *Peresopnytsia Gospel*] has been used to administer the Oath of Office to the country's Presidents.'

The paintings, which feature unorthodox iconography, an original layout of different episodes, and expressive lines in some compositions, also contain inscriptions in Latin.

The everyday culture of the era required residents of western Ukrainian lands to have a basic command of several languages. Yurii Donat-Kotermak, who became rector of the University of Bologna, was, in many ways, an exceptional individual, and his life is proof that a western Ukrainian native could succeed in Rome. In 1483, Kotermak published his incunabula (an early type of book or pamphlet) *Iudicium Pronosticon Anni 1483 Currentis*, in which he described 'The Kingdom of Rus' as belonging firmly within European territory.

From the multilingualism of everyday life emerged a contemporary school of translation. The *Peresopnytsia Gospel* of the sixteenth century represents one of the first Ukrainian translations of the canonical Gospels from the Church Slavonic of a Bulgarian original into Old Ukrainian, the vernacular language of sermons delivered to the public. Made from 1556 to 1561 by Mykhailo Vasylovych from Sianik and Hryhorii, the archimandrite of the Peresopnytsia Monastery, the text incorporates borrowings from Greek and Polish sources. The sponsors of the translation were the Volhynian princess Anastasiia Zaslavska, her daughter Yevdokiia, and her son-in-law Prince Ivan Fedorovych Chortoryiski. Their generous funding enabled the anonymous illustrators to produce a luxurious volume adorned with natural imagery, which is also characteristic of Italian Mannerist art. The style visually connects the manuscript with the carved doorways of contemporary Lviv townhouses. The regularity of the lettering in the Gospel is evidence of the high level of scriptorial expertise, preserved in monastic scriptoria by copying Kyivan originals from prior centuries. The bright, active colours of the illustration and the abundant gilding attest to the artists' desire to reinterpret the canonical Byzantine aesthetic. In 1701 Hetman Ivan Mazepa gave this book as a gift to Pereiaslav Cathedral. Mazepa was the first public figure to realize that important artistic relics should be promoted in order to increase their significance beyond a single region of Ukraine. The Gospel, bound between a modest set of oak boards covered in green velvet, is today considered a national treasure and, since the declaration of Ukraine's independence in 1991, has been used to administer the Oath of Office to the country's Presidents.

Despite the high quality of hand-written books, the future – including that of Ukrainian education – lay with a new technology: printing. The richest magnates and patrons of the time understood the importance of this transition. The first complete

11
Peresopnytsia Gospel
1561
Made in Volhynia
Vernadskyi National Library
of Ukraine, Kyiv

printed translation of the Bible into Church Slavonic, undertaken by a committee of scholars at the Ostroh School and published in 1580–81 with funding provided by Count Kostiantyn Vasyl Ostrozkyi, is known today as the *Ostroh Bible* (Fig. 12, p. 100). Ivan Fedorovych, a printer working in Lviv who published the book, is considered to be the German inventor, printer, and publisher Johannes Gutenberg's Slavic peer. Fedorovych had to create several new typefaces (four in Cyrillic, and two in Greek, of different sizes) as well as all graphic embellishments for the volume. The book consists of 628 pages with filigree by Busk paper-making workshops, coats of arms, and ornamental frames and initials based on examples provided by the Venetian printer Aldo Manuzio. With its masterful typesetting and high-quality printing, the book is a model of graphic harmony. In the process of translating the book, the committee collected copies of the Bible from across Europe and cross-checked them against the Greek Septuagint. They also added a foreword by their patron, poems by the Ostroh School rector Herasym Smotrytskyi, and a short afterword by Ivan Fedorovych. Clearly, the creators of the book understood that they were setting

'With its masterful typesetting and high-quality printing, the book is a model of graphic harmony.'

12
Ostroh Bible
1580–81
Made in Volhynia
Vernadskyi National Library
of Ukraine, Kyiv

a historic precedent. The exact print-run is not known, but experts believe it was significant for its time, as large as two thousand copies. More than 350 copies exist in libraries, museums, and private collections around the world.

To imagine the potential buyer for such an expensive volume as the one conceived by the Ostroh team, we can refer to the *Portrait of a Man in a Red Coat*. The subject of the painting, a solidly built man with an attentive expression, opted for a portrait in the Sarmatian style – rather than an icon – for his dwelling. True, he had to settle for a more modest, half-length version than what was available to contemporary princes and lesser nobles, but it is telling that he could afford to commission such a piece in the first place.

The Wealthy Cities
of Magdeburg Law

International trade, which facilitated the exchange not only of goods, but also of art objects, contributed to a dynamic environment in which styles could change, new genres could emerge, and fresh themes could be explored. Kostiantyn Korniakt, a Lviv wine merchant originally from Crete, exemplifies the kind of individual who invested in the transfer of valuables, in architecture, and in many artworks for his own home. Korniakt was granted noble status for his loyal service as a personal secretary to the King of Poland Sigismund II Augustus. The next king, Stephen Báthory, issued a special decree in 1576 to allow Korniakt to build a family residence, six windows in width, in Lviv's Market Square. Most townhouses around the square were constructed to be three windows wide, and the privilege of exceeding this allocation was granted only as a reward for the most distinguished service. The Korniakt Palace (Fig. 15, pp. 104–5) of the Renaissance period retained a Gothic-style grand hall, now the only example of secular Gothic architecture in Ukraine. An Italianate courtyard modelled on the Renaissance atria of Florence and Rome became the most admired feature of the palace. It is sometimes called the Venetian courtyard because the space retains its authentic windows, commissioned by Korniakt and created by Murano craftsmen. When the Italian adventurer and author Giacomo Casanova visited Lviv, the courtyard hosted performances of Shakespeare's plays.

'When the Italian adventurer and author Giacomo Casanova visited Lviv, the courtyard [of Korniakt Palace] hosted performances of Shakespeare's plays.'

The palace's street façade features the inscriptions '27 AP 1580' and 'MPEB' above the Renaissance-style doorway. These refer to the date when work was completed and are signed with the name of the architect, Murator Petrus Barbon. It is possible that Barbon was assisted by his student, the Italian Pavlo Rymlianyn, whom Korniakt would later commission to build the city's tallest tower. Korniakta Tower resembles the bell tower of Santo Stefano in Venice, and still bears Korniakt's name.

Residents of those cities with Magdeburg rights enjoyed significant economic benefits, and these rights spread fairly far to the east. Magistrates protected the guilds from feudal encroachments, set the places and terms of trade, and organized trade fairs, some of which became international. Kyiv, for instance, at the end of the fifteenth century, made use of two magisterial seals. The first, about 25 mm in diameter, was applied to local contracts, while the larger one, 41 mm in diameter and with the Latin inscription CAPI CIVITA TERRA KIOVIE ('Seal of the capital city of the Kyiv land'; Fig. 14), functioned as the state seal. Soviet historians believed that after the 1482 sacking by the forces of the Crimean Khanate led by Mengli I Giray (who acted at the bidding of Moscow's Prince Ivan III), when Kyiv's wooden castle was burned and its churches ransacked, the city remained in ruins for a long time. However, the existence of these seals contradicts such a version of events, and points instead to the continued development of the city, which, by the early seventeenth century, featured not only international trading fairs, but also printing houses and a confraternity school that would soon become the Kyiv-Mohyla Academy.

14
Seal of the city of Kyiv
First half of 16th century
Copper alloy
Height 35 mm; diameter 41 mm
Sheremetiev Museum, Kyiv

15 (*overleaf*)
Korniakt Palace
16th century
Lviv

In the west of Ukraine, the largest centre of traditional arts and crafts was the city of Kosiv (Ivano-Frankivsk oblast), best known for its ceramics – especially the production of ceramic stove tiles, famous for their simple yet expressive images and recognizable beige and green colour scheme.

In Soviet times, specialized factories were opened for production in many
of the cities noted for their folk crafts. [...] After the collapse of the USSR,
production was mainly continued by individual artist-entrepreneurs.
See page 242.

THE BAROQUE ERA

17th and 18th centuries

Maksym Yaremenko

At the beginning of the seventeenth century, most Ukrainian lands were part of the federated Polish–Lithuanian Commonwealth, one of the largest states in Europe. The multi-ethnic Commonwealth was remarkable for its religious tolerance. An elected parliament limited the power of the monarch, and local councils (*sejms*) were an important feature of the nation's political life. Ukrainian (or Ruthenian) nobility (*szlachta*) embodied knightly culture and enjoyed the full spectrum of political rights. Until the middle of the seventeenth century, this social group was not only clearly aware of its unique political identity, but also identified itself as the third member-people of the Commonwealth, along with the Poles and the Lithuanians.

During the first half of the seventeenth century, the processes of urbanization, colonization, and domestication of the southern and southeastern borderlands continued throughout Ukrainian lands. Religious and cultural life were driven by interconfessional discussions. While Orthodox believers dominated the religious map of the land, it was during this time that the Uniate (later called Greek Catholic) Church formally emerged, following the Union of Brest in 1596 in which the Kyiv Metropolitanate separated from the Orthodox Church and joined Rome. Roman Catholic institutions continued their centuries-old activities, the Protestant movement was strong, and Jewish and Muslim groups practised their respective faiths. The so-called patronage right became an important social, cultural, and religious norm: each landowner was expected, in accordance with the virtues of a 'good lord', to patronize subjects of different religions and confessions. For example, the city of Ostroh, the residence of the powerful Ruthenian prince and senator Kostiantyn Ostrozkyi, was home to Orthodox, Catholic, and Lutheran churches, along with an Arian church, a mosque, and a synagogue. At the same time, Prince Ostrozkyi himself was a devoted Orthodox believer and did much to support the Orthodox Church in its competition with the Uniates. Town residents also took an active part in social and ecclesiastical affairs: they shared with the clergy responsibilities and funding for education and book-printing, and organized their own faith-based confraternities (brotherhoods). Kyiv, the ancient Ruthenian capital, regained its population following attacks by Crimean Tatars in the late fifteenth century, and alongside Lviv, increased its cultural, religious, and political significance.

Zaporizhian Cossacks also began to emerge as a political force at the beginning of the seventeenth century (see Chapter 3). At that time, there was no official 'Cossack state'; the Cossacks were subjects of the Polish–Lithuanian Commonwealth, but they were assigned territory and owned lands. They elected their own leaders, and had their own seal, flag, and other regalia. Armed Cossack forces gradually turned into a well-organized military community that lived by its own unwritten rules and traditions. The Polish king relied on their military skill to defend the Commonwealth border and to fight the Ottoman Empire, Muscovy, and the Swedes.

page 108
Yov Kondzelevych
Icon of the Archangel
Gabriel of the Bohorodchany
Iconostasis (detail)
c. 1698–1705
See Fig. 4a, p. 119

Cossack demands were constantly expanding. They increasingly interfered in church and city affairs in the border areas. Uprisings occurred following violations of their rights, such as reductions of their officially recognized numbers, non-payment for military campaigns, or interference by other administrations in Cossack affairs. In this way, they slowly became a separate social state with their own rights and responsibilities. The Cossack uprising of 1648, led by Bohdan Khmelnytskyi (c. 1595–1657), began with a stand against the violation of Khmelnytskyi's personal rights and rapidly developed into a revolution. Disenfranchised commoners flocked *en masse* to the banner of the Cossacks' struggle for their special status (since the landowners who ruled over the poor opposed the Cossacks), and a portion of burghers and *szlachta* also joined. Khmelnytskyi legitimated his insurgence by claiming he was acting in defence of the Orthodox faith. This allowed the Cossacks to speak on behalf of all Ruthenian Orthodox people and to seek support from the Orthodox tsar in Moscow. In 1654, Khmelnytskyi accepted the protection of the Moscow tsar. Reared in the political traditions of the Commonwealth, where the king was elected, the Cossacks expected this pact to bring protection and preserve their existing privileges. Muscovy, however, treated the agreement as an acknowledgment of the Cossacks' unconditional fealty to the tsar. Once this became clear, Khmelnytskyi attempted to switch his alliance to the Swedish king. The Cossacks were also in negotiations with other neighbouring powers – the Ottomans and the Tatars among them.

After Khmelnytskyi's death, different factions of the Cossacks that advocated for different alliances – with the Commonwealth, Muscovy, or the Ottoman Empire – plunged into an internecine struggle supported by neighbours. This period, which caused great demographic and economic losses, is known as 'The Ruin' and lasted until 1687 when Ivan Mazepa became Hetman, a position he held until 1709. During his Hetmanate, the territorial boundaries of the Cossack jurisdiction were settled and formalized. New treaties with the Russian state and the Commonwealth did not honour the Cossacks' wishes and divided the Ukrainian lands approximately along the Dnipro. The right bank, except for a small territory near Kyiv, remained under Commonwealth control. Kyiv, including its right-bank suburbs, and all lands to the east of the Dnipro, were ceded to the Russian state.

The Cossack revolution and the loss of so many Ukrainian voivodeships (administrative regions) weakened the Commonwealth significantly. From the second half of the seventeenth century, the state was no longer as tolerant of different religions. By the early eighteenth century, there were no Orthodox eparchies left in the Ukrainian voivodeships, and only individual monasteries and parishes were allowed to function. The lion's share of Ukrainians joined the Uniate Church. In this manner, the border between the Commonwealth and the Russian state also became a confessional divide.

By the end of the eighteenth century, the Polish–Lithuanian Commonwealth was divided up by its more powerful neighbours. Muscovy, enlarged by the addition of Ukrainian lands, gained political as well as territorial weight. The tsars were now able to exploit the economic and human resources of the fertile Ukrainian lands. The Cossacks were deployed in every important war of the emergent Russian Empire, and Ukrainian religious thinkers modernized Russia's Church and education system.

The Cossack revolution of 1648 brought about the Cossack Hetmanate (*Hetmanshchyna*), an autonomous state-like polity. Here, Cossacks became the new *res publica*, the enfranchised political class, like the Commonwealth *szlachta*. The Hetmanate was a single-faith society, limited to the Orthodox Church. The Orthodox Metropolitan of Kyiv was subject to the Patriarch of Constantinople until 1686, when the Patriarch of Moscow, in violation of canonical law, extended his jurisdiction to Kyiv. In the second half of the seventeenth century, another region inhabited by the Cossacks but separate and independent of the Hetmanate, Slobozhanshchyna, emerged in the Russian–Ukrainian ethnic borderlands as a result of Ukrainian colonization. Despite being under the tsars' rule (after 1721, the Russian emperors'), the Hetmanate preserved its own social order, governance, legal practices, and worldview until the end of the eighteenth century. These, to a large extent, were based on Commonwealth norms: the knightly culture of the Cossacks was formed there.

Centralization reforms by the Russian Tsar Peter the Great threatened the Hetmanate's autonomy and implied the eradication of the Cossacks as a privileged social class. Therefore, Hetman Ivan Mazepa opposed the Russian monarch and made an alliance with the Swedish King Karl XII, supporting Sweden in the Great Northern War. The defeat of the joint Swedish–Cossack forces at Poltava in 1709 brought on Russian persecution of the Hetman's circle and a further restriction of Hetmanate rights. Throughout the eighteenth century, the tsars' attitude toward Cossack autonomy vacillated depending on how urgently the throne needed the Cossack military force. Finally, Catherine the Great instituted unification reforms that ended the Hetmanate's existence. Nonetheless, in the modern nation-building era, Cossack autonomy has become a symbol of Ukrainian sovereignty.

The political and religious division of Ukrainian lands did not mean there was an impenetrable barrier between them. Neighbours who were subjects of different countries continued to interact with each other. Family ties, pilgrimages, business, and smuggling continued, along with every other form of cross-border movement.

Ukrainian culture of the seventeenth to eighteenth century developed in keeping with wider trends in Europe. The Baroque period brought new ways of thinking and new architecture, literature, and art. Religion continued to be integral to Ukrainian culture, and within the Commonwealth the cultural context remained multi-religious, multicultural, and multilingual. Educated leaders of the Hetmanate and Slobozhanshchyna were also multilingual and well versed in western European thought through their education, travels, and imported books. Thanks to Kyivan intellectuals, Ukrainian culture synthesized eastern (Byzantine) and western (Latin) Christianity into a unique identity. It was also during this period that the Ukrainian early-modern nation emerged, as the Hetmanate political elites developed a premodern national identity.

St George's wooden church, interior
See Fig. 3, p. 118

Third Member of the Republic of Two Nations

Both within the Polish–Lithuanian Commonwealth and the Russian Empire, Ukrainian lands had the reputation of an endlessly fertile Klondike. Polish magnates and *szlachta* began colonizing and domesticating the southern and southeastern Ukrainian frontiers as early as the second half of the sixteenth century. By the middle of the seventeenth century, approximately a quarter of all landholdings there belonged to immigrant landowners. Large estates grew grain, which was exported to western Europe through the main port of the trade, Gdansk. The new landowners and their client Poles were initially perceived as foreigners. With the help of marriage diplomacy, however, they built family ties with the native Ruthenian nobility, and with time, came to hold posts in local governments. At the same time, many of the Ukrainian magnates converted to the more prestigious Catholicism.

The large Polish Potocki (Potoskyi) family owned many estates in different parts of Ukraine. In the eighteenth century, the family invested in porcelain factories, cloth mills, and carriage-building enterprises in the town they owned. In addition to castles, palatial estates (which came to displace fortified estates in the eighteenth century), and churches, another material proof of the Potoskyis' political, cultural, and land-management efforts is represented by the landscape park Sofiivka, founded in the eighteenth century on the outskirts of Uman. Similarly, the town hall in Buchach (from the mid-eighteenth century) belongs among the treasures of the Ukrainian Baroque. The building's construction was funded by the Kaniv *starosta* (the highest administrative and judicial office in the administrative unit called the *starostvo*), Mykola Vasyl Potoskyi (d. 1782), Knight of the Order of Malta, who owned Buchach, in addition to many other towns and landholdings on Ukrainian and Polish territories. Potoskyi gave generously to the cause of the Uniate Church and education in general, and even converted to the Greek Catholic faith himself. During his lifetime, Mykola Vasyl Potoskyi's figure was the subject of many legends and rumours. It was said, for instance, that he killed a young woman who refused his advances, and later, to atone for this transgression, sponsored the building of dozens of churches.

The Buchach Town Hall is the work of Bernard Meretyn (d. 1759), an architect of either Austrian or German origin. Meretyn was so popular in Lviv that he ran afoul of the local master-builders, who accused him of unfair competition. The two-storey façade, more than 35 metres tall, was decorated with sculptures of biblical characters and figures of Classical mythology. Such an evidently odd mixture of Christian and pagan motifs was characteristic of the Baroque era. These stone carvings were made by Johann Georg Pinsel, an immigrant of unknown origin, who was also famous for his work in wood. Both he and Meretyn took in many pupils while they worked for Potoskyi.

Meretyn and Pinsel also collaborated on the residence of the Lviv Uniate Metropolitans, St George's Cathedral (Fig. 2, pp. 116–17). The cathedral was built

1
Buchach Town Hall
Bernard Meretyn (architect) and Johann Georg Pinsel (sculptures)
1740–50
Buchach, Ternopil oblast

2 (*overleaf*)
St George's Cathedral
Bernard Meretyn and Klemens Fesinger (architects) and Johann Georg Pinsel (sculptures)
1744–61
Lviv

between 1744 and 1761, but decorative work was not finished until the late 1770s. After Meretyn's death, Klemens Fesinger, another architect of German birth, took over. Pinsel's works adorn the cathedral's façades. At the time of the cathedral's construction, less than fifty years had passed since the Lviv eparchy, previously Orthodox, converted to the Union, and the task of building its most important church proved to be a challenge. In the eighteenth century, the Greek Catholic ecclesiastical hierarchy undertook an entire programme of religious education for its clergy and laity. Architecture, too, was called upon to express the special identity of the church, with its eastern roots and its alignment with Rome. The church leadership wanted this structure, set in Lviv's multicultural environment, to emphasize the unique Greek Catholic religious identity, distinct from both Roman Catholic and Orthodox ones. The new cathedral was also intended to underscore the equal standing of the Greek Catholic faith (which was often said to be 'the peasant church') with Roman Catholicism. It had, therefore, to look both luxurious and contemporary. The problem was the persistent scarcity of local master-builders who could work in stone. A handful of architects, invited from abroad, designed and built churches of different faiths, as well as synagogues, and all these buildings, as a result, shared several architectural features and often resembled their western European peers.

The vast majority of religious buildings in Ukraine were at the time built of wood and erected by local master-builders. Stone-builders were a rarity, not to be found at all in some towns. The wooden, three-nave churches, which differ regionally in certain structural details, were cheaper, built of a more accessible material, and portable (they could be sold, transported, and reassembled on a new site). The main challenge of such churches is their quick deterioration. To withstand the elements, wooden churches require repairs or even partial reconstruction every few decades – this is

3
St George's wooden church
15th century; rebuilt 1650
Drohobych, Lviv oblast

why so few of them survive to this day. Among the preserved examples is St George's Church in Drohobych, rebuilt in 1650. Representatives of the same family served as priests of the church from the beginning of the sixteenth to the end of the seventeenth century; during the eighteenth century, another family enjoyed the same privilege. Such changes do not necessarily indicate that the priest's family owned the church, as approval of the priest was the patron's prerogative.

Wood was used in other types of construction as well: most of the residential and commercial infrastructure was built of wood, and wood was laid down as the pavement, for example, on some of Kyiv's streets in the seventeenth and eighteenth centuries. Fires in this time were therefore frequent and potentially catastrophic: fires destroyed libraries, archives, and works of art, as well as buildings and property.

Ukrainian painting of the seventeenth and eighteenth centuries is best represented in icons. Most works dating from the seventeenth century came from or were painted in western Ukraine. Their artists were Ukrainian, Polish, and Armenian. From the late sixteenth century, Lviv played a trend-setting role in the industry, along with the town of Zhovkva, where Ivan Rutkovych (d. early 1700s) worked (Fig. 4b). This was also the birthplace of Yov Kondzelevych (1667–1740), creator of the enormous Baroque Bohorodchany Iconostasis (Fig. 4a shows one panel). Works of high art could not possibly satisfy the popular demand for icons, since every Christian was expected to have a few in their residence. For this reason, so-called 'folk painters' also produced icons, and in the eighteenth century icons printed on paper made their first appearance.

Cossack *Patria*

Bohdan Khmelnytskyi, to whom the Hetmanate owes its emergence, was an extraordinary individual. His contemporaries described him as a powerful and authoritative leader who preferred to lead a simple life. Khmelnytskyi came from a minor *szlachta* family and studied at the Jesuit collegium in Lviv. At the time, plenty of Orthodox youth took advantage of the high-quality education the Jesuit institutions offered for free and of their tolerance toward students of non-Catholic faith. The future Hetman also had direct military experience earned during his days as a Cossack and was even captured and held captive for a time by the Ottomans. Some scholars believe that in 1649, during the second year of the Cossack uprising, Khmelnytskyi received a message of support from Oliver Cromwell.

The spark that lit the fire of the uprising that would redraw the political map of east-central Europe was an attack by Khmelnytskyi's neighbour on his estate in the village of Subotiv, involving the murder of his son and imprisonment of his wife. Later, the Hetman himself would be buried in Subotiv in the chapel he built for his family in St Illia's Church. The village then became an important site for Cossack memory. According to one version of the events, the stone used to build Khmelnytskyi's chapel was recycled from a ruined mosque nearby.

The rulers of this new polity – Hetmans and the Cossack elite who governed the Hetmanate – were, as behoved the powerful of the contemporary world,

5
St Illia's Church
1653
Subotiv, Cherkasy oblast

6
Kyiv-Pecherska Lavra
11th to 18th century
UNESCO World Heritage Site

'By the end of the sixteenth century, records show [the Lavra had] a well-developed pilgrimage "industry", including a visitor management procedure, with a suggested route, donations, and recommended rituals.'

generous patrons of the Orthodox Church. They funded the building of new churches and renovations of the old ones, now reborn in Baroque architecture.

The Kyiv-Pecherska Lavra (Fig. 6, p. 121) is the best known of the Ukrainian Orthodox ensembles. The Lavra was established back in the eleventh century, and its first above-ground stone buildings can be dated to the eleventh and twelfth centuries. In the first half of the eighteenth century, the monastery's buildings acquired their current Baroque forms. Both within the Polish–Lithuanian Commonwealth and later in the Hetmanate, the Lavra enjoyed vast support and exercised great influence on monarchs and the nobility, and was famous for its extraordinary riches. An elite necropolis formed within its walls and the monastery attracted thousands of pilgrims from across eastern Europe every year. Pilgrims and other foreigners were drawn by the reputation of this holy site, evidenced by the incorruptible remains of dozens of saints interred in the ancient caves under the monastery. By the end of the sixteenth century, records show a well-developed pilgrimage 'industry', including a visitor management procedure, with a suggested route, donations, and recommended rituals. One of Ukraine's biggest printing houses began operating in the Lavra in about 1615, producing books in both Latin and Cyrillic alphabets. The monastery successfully defended its monopoly on book printing, enhanced by its own bookshop in Kyiv, until the end of the eighteenth century. The Lavra's icon-painting school was also well known and attracted students from other lands, especially Serbia.

Hetman Ivan Mazepa was one of the most significant patrons of the Lavra. There is even a legend, recorded in the nineteenth century, that holds that Mazepa did not actually die in 1709 in Bendery in Moldova, where he emigrated after the defeat of his uprising against the Russian tsar, but secretly made his way to Kyiv and lived out his days as a Lavra monk.

Baroque icon-paining is predominantly represented by eighteenth-century examples, with many well-preserved iconostases. In the post-Mazepa Hetmanate, icons became a vehicle for political messages. Political elites communicated their sense of identity and their aspirations through specific images included in the icons. One of these such politically tinted icons – the icon showing the Intercession of the Theotokos, from the first half of the eighteenth century – includes the image of Bohdan Khmelnytskyi (Fig. 7). This reference to the founder of the Cossack state not only demonstrates his status as a cult figure, but also reminds the viewer that the Ukrainian elites remembered their rights and privileges won in the revolution of the seventeenth century and insisted on their special status within the Russian Empire. More broadly, the cult of the Intercession of the Theotokos was very popular in contemporary Ukrainian culture.

'Political elites communicated their sense of identity and their aspirations through specific images included in the icons.'

Many more stone religious buildings than secular buildings survive from the Hetmanate era. The latter were usually modest, one-storey buildings. Still, individual Hetmans' palaces and the residences of church leadership stood out, if not in terms of their refinement and adornment, then at least in size and interior comfort. One such example is the residence of the Kyiv Metropolitans (the mansard added in the 1750s; Fig. 8). Kyiv, although it was the largest city of Cossack Ukraine, in which the fluctuating population in the eighteenth century could sometimes reach forty thousand, was not the Hetmanate's capital. The large Russian garrison and powerful city government left Cossacks feeling ill-at-ease here. Nonetheless, the city remained the most important religious centre, and the Kyiv Metropolitan occupied the oldest, and chief, ecclesiastical throne in the Russian Empire.

The new Cossack and church elite in Kyiv and Left-bank Ukraine (a region on the east bank of the Dnipro River) supported the development of portrait painting, often in the form of *ktitor* (donor) and epitaph paintings, which had previously been less widespread than icon painting or the secular portraiture of the Polish–Lithuanian Commonwealth. One of the very few examples of early portraiture in the Hetmanate is the late-seventeenth century portrait of the Cossack leader Hryhorii Hamaliia, painted during his life. Hamaliia (d. 1702) lived during the time of 'The Ruin' and served a number of Hetmans, including as the Cossack ambassador to Turkey and Muscovy. He fought in several campaigns, assisted Ivan Mazepa's rise to power (and was, for a time, in opposition to Mazepa), and owned significant landholdings. The portrait is executed in the Sarmatian *szlachta* genre, distinguished, among other features, by the emphasis on the sitter's substantial physique, the typical pose, and the decorative element. The existence of such portraits in the Hetmanate shows that the Cossack elite adopted models of visual self-representation that were typical of the Commonwealth nobility.

8
Metropolitan's Residence, St Sophia's
1722–57
Kyiv

Anonymous
Portrait of Hryhorii Hamaliia
18th century
oil on canvas
133.5 × 85 cm
National Art Museum
of Ukraine, Kyiv

'Kyiv, although it was the largest city of Cossack
Ukraine [...] was not the Hetmanate's capital. The
large Russian garrison and powerful city government
left Cossacks feeling ill-at-ease here.'

The University Tradition

By the middle of the seventeenth century, a well-developed network of educational institutions spread across Ukraine: there were fifteen Jesuit collegiums, nearly a dozen Calvinist and Socinian colleges, and a handful of Uniate (whose peak would come in the second half of the eighteenth century) and Orthodox schools. Among the latter, the confraternal school in Kyiv, founded in 1615, was the most important; Latin was also taught there. It was this school that the Orthodox hierarch Petro Mohyla (1596/7–1647; see Fig. 11) reformed in 1632, instituting the humanistic model of education already practised across Europe and specifically by the Jesuits. In 1658, the Kyiv school received from the Polish–Lithuanian Commonwealth authority rights equal to those of the Kraków Academy and became the first *de jure* university in Ukrainian lands (it would remain the most eastern university of Europe until the middle of the eighteenth century). However, the academy failed to exercise its rights to self-governance fully once Kyiv became part of the Russian Empire, where the European university tradition was entirely unknown. The language of instruction in the Kyiv-Mohyla Academy was Latin; Polish, Greek, and Hebrew were also taught, with German added in 1738, French in 1753, and Russian in 1784 (until the end of the eighteenth century, Ukrainians did not study and, with few exceptions, did not speak Russian). More than one thousand students of all social backgrounds attended the Academy each year. They came not only from Ukraine, but also from Belarusian, Serbian, Bulgarian, Montenegrin, Russian, Moldovan, and Greek lands. Many alumni of the Academy went on to significant ecclesiastical and secular careers. Ivan Mazepa attended the Kyiv-Mohyla Academy, as well as his aide and successor, and eventual

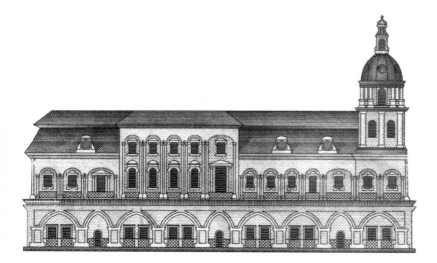

10
Reconstruction drawing of the Old Academy (Mazepa) building
1704–39
Kyiv

1
Anonymous
Portrait of Kyiv and Halych
Metropolitan Petro Mohyla
Second half of 18th century
National Art Museum of Ukraine,
Kyiv

ПЕТРЪ МОГИЛА. ВОЕВОДИЧЪ ЗЕМЛИ МОЛДАВСКОИ
АРХИМАНДРИТЪ ПЕЧЕРСКIИ МИТРОПОЛИТЪ КIЕВСКIИ. ПРЕСТАВИСѦ АХМЗ

political emigrant Pylyp Orlyk; so did the first Ukrainian lay philosopher Hryhorii Skovoroda; Theophan Prokopovich, the ideologist of imperial reforms; Prince Alexander Bezborodko, the Grand Chancellor of the Russian Empire; the epidemiologist and doctor of medicine Danylo Samoilovych, member of twelve European academies; composer Artem Vedel; Constantius I, the Patriarch of Constantinople; and hundreds of other renowned individuals. The Kyiv-Mohyla Academy alumni founded dozens of schools in Ukraine and beyond. In 1819, the Academy was updated into a modern institution of higher religious education. The main building, partially reconstructed in the nineteenth century, is still used as originally intended. It was finished in the late 1730s, but an engraving by the well-known Ukrainian artist Inokentii Shchyrskyi, dating from between 1697 and 1701, shows that plans for this two-storey building already existed then.

Petro Mohyla's educational reforms represent only one of his many efforts. As the Metropolitan of Kyiv (1633–47), Mohyla, who came from a blue-blooded family of Moldovan rulers, belonged to a new generation of Europe's post-Reformation religious leaders, ambitious in their education, worldview and aspirations. Mohyla professionalized the clergy and educated the laity; he unified liturgical practice, cultivated a strong faith-based identity, and supported the intellectual growth of the Church. As a result of his reforms, the Kyiv Metropolitanatebecame one of the most powerful centres of the Orthodox world.

'More than one thousand students of all social backgrounds attended the Academy each year. They came not only from Ukraine, but also from Belarusian, Serbian, Bulgarian, Montenegrin, Russian, Moldovan, and Greek lands.'

Polyconfessionalism and Multiculturalism

In the seventeenth and eighteenth centuries, many ethnic and religious groups made their homes in the lands of today's Ukraine. Among them were Poles, Armenians, Germans, Tatars, and Greeks. The first small groups of Russians came to settle in the Hetmanate in the eighteenth century. By the middle of the seventeenth century, there were as many as 150,000 Jews in central and eastern Ukraine. During the Cossack uprising, this group, along with Roman Catholics, became associated with the Cossack's religious and social enemies – landholders and their allies. Jewish people were banned from establishing permanent residency in the Hetmanate and could only enter temporarily (for example, as merchants). Those who converted from Judaism to Christianity were treated without any further bias, and some such individuals integrated into the Cossack elite and ecclesiastical hierarchy. Both Judaism and the Roman Catholic Church left notable imprints on the cultural landscape of the Ukrainian voivodeships of the Polish–Lithuanian Commonwealth. Meanwhile, in the Ukrainian lands under Russian control, Orthodox Christianity ruled supreme.

The Ukrainian oblast of Podillia became in the eighteenth century the cradle of Hasidism, whose adherents today live all over the world. The founder of the movement, Rabbi Israel ben Eliezer (c. 1700–60), also known as the Baal Shem Tov, or Besht, lived and died in Medzhybizh, and was renowned as a healer and a teacher. The new movement's followers believed that through prayer and mystical intellectual

2
Husiatyn Synagogue
17th century
Husiatyn, Ternopil oblast

contemplation they could interact with the divine, promoting pious life and efforts to increase joy. Among well-known Jewish historical structures in Ukraine is the seventeenth-century synagogue in the town of Husiatyn, built in the fortified style with Moorish features (Fig. 12, p. 129).

The Roman Catholic Monastery of Discalced Carmelites in Berdychiv, founded in the first half of the seventeenth century, became an important cultural and religious centre. The founder, Janusz Tyszkiewicz, came from an ancient and wealthy *szlachta* family from the Kyiv region. The monastery's St Mary's Cathedral patronized religious confraternities, supported a chapel, and, from the end of the eighteenth century, schools. The Carmelites' wide renown came from the miracle-working icon of the Virgin, Our Lady of Berdychiv, which attracted great numbers of pilgrims, as well as its publishing house (active between 1758 and 1844). More than one thousand titles came off the Carmelite presses, most in Polish and Latin, but also in French, German, and Russian – 499 of these were published before the end of the eighteenth century. In addition to religious tracts, the workshop published secular histories, works of literature, and textbooks. Of special renown across Ukraine were the Berdychiv calendars: annual almanacs, published by the thousands and filled with religious, historical, and reference information (e.g. on contemporary European monarchs and important bureaucrats) as well as farming advice.

In the Orthodox Church in the seventeenth and eighteenth centuries, the figure of the Apostle Andrii (Andrew) acquired special significance. According to legend, Andrii planted a cross on the Dnipro River bluffs on the site of today's Kyiv and prophesied that a great city would arise there, from which Christianity would spread. The Kyiv Metropolitanate considered the apostle its founder and the most important of the apostles. In various interconfessional disputes of the early seventeenth century, appeals to such great authority allowed the Kyiv Church to defend itself against allegations of lacking legitimacy and to emphasize its apostolic origins. In 1744,

13
Monastery of the Discalced Carmelites
First half of 17th century
Berdychiv, Zhytomyr oblast

foundations were laid for a stone church on the site where legend holds that the Apostle Andrii planted his cross. The Russian Empress Elizabeth Petrovna herself contributed to the project. There was already a wooden church on the same site, dating back to the thirteenth century. Known as the Church of the Exaltation of the Holy Cross, it was ruined and rebuilt several times, and finally reconsecrated to Andrew the Apostle in 1690. In 1724, this wooden building collapsed. The change of name at the end of the seventeenth century was no coincidence: not long beforehand, the Moscow Patriarch annexed the Kyiv Metropolitanate. The religious elites of Kyiv used the apostle's name yet again to remind Moscow of Kyiv's primacy as a religious centre and its ancient ties to Constantinople (Andrew is believed to be Constantinople's first Patriarch).

Work on the stone church began in 1747, under the patronage of the Imperial throne. However, after 1761, Petersburg lost interest in the project, and the consecration of the church took place without the pomp that had accompanied the laying of its cornerstone. The architect of the building was Francesco Bartolomeo Rastrelli, an Italian architect in Russian service. Rastrelli never came to Kyiv and was not familiar with the site, whose peculiarities – the ground-water level and constant ground slippages – became the building's perennial challenges. Immediately after the church was completed in the late 1760s, it required structural renovations. Since then, the church itself or the hill it stands on were reinforced once more in the eighteenth century, four times in the nineteenth century, and six times in the twentieth century – such work is likely to continue.

Embroidery is one of the most common forms of decoration in traditional Ukrainian textiles. Typical embroidered items in Ukrainian art include womens' and men's shirts, as well as towels. Richly embroidered towels were an important design feature in folk interiors, as well as playing a role in folk rituals and as part of a bride's dowry. The collections of Ukrainian museums contain many wonderful examples of the country's folk embroidery from the early eighteenth to the twentieth centuries.

A significant number of geometric ornamental motifs, which once held allusions to magic, have been preserved in Ukrainian embroidery. In parallel with old abstract patterns, new, more realistic elements – mainly floral – gradually appeared in embroidered designs. A characteristic feature of folk embroidery is the variety of techniques, frequently applied in combination. Traditionally, embroidery threads were coloured with natural dyes made of tree bark, leaves, flowers, and fruits. See page 242.

THE NINETEENTH CENTURY & THE FIN-DE-SIÈCLE

1800 to 1917

Alisa Lozhkina

U krainian art of the nineteenth and early twentieth centuries is inextricably linked to the country's history of the period. Ukraine entered the nineteenth century in a fragmented state. After the Third Partition of the Polish–Lithuanian Commonwealth in 1795, western Ukraine was divided between the Austrian and Russian empires. The lands east of the Dnipro River had been allied with the Tsardom of Russia since the second half of the seventeenth century, and by the time the Russian Empire was formed in the eighteenth century, these lands had become its *de facto* colony. As the nineteenth century began, it seemed that all traces of the Khmelnytskyi Uprising of 1648 to 1654 and the heroic past of the Cossack Hetmanate had been completely erased from memory. Ukraine effectively became the western outpost of the Russian Empire.

Following the Russo-Turkish war (1768–74), lands in the lower reaches of the Dnipro River, seaports around the Azov Sea, and then Crimea were ceded by the Ottoman Empire to the Russian Empire. By the turn of the century, the region had been colonized by migrants from other parts of Ukraine, as well as by people of different nationalities – Bulgarians, Greeks, Moldovans, and others – who fled to these emptier, far-away lands that had relatively greater freedom. In the south, new cities appeared: Katerynoslav (present-day Dnipro), Mykolaiv, Kherson, Odesa, Sevastopol, and Mariupol, all of which were actively built up and developed in the nineteenth century. Kyiv, too, grew significantly. The need for functional, harmonious urban areas led to an increase in the number and, gradually, the quality of architectural projects being built. At the end of the eighteenth and beginning of the nineteenth centuries, classicism dominated in architecture. An example of this style is the Kyiv Arsenal (1784–1801), a huge, almost square structure built as part of the defensive fortifications of the Kyiv Fortress. Today, this historic building houses the largest museum and exhibition complex in Ukraine – the Mystetskyi Arsenal.

To strengthen the western borders of the vast Russian Empire, local liberties were suppressed, particularly in areas where imperial authority was more fragile. In 1775, by order of Empress Catherine II, the Zaporizhian Sich (the stronghold of the Cossack state) was disbanded. The former Cossack elite was gradually Russified and integrated into the imperial structure. By the beginning of the nineteenth century, the elite were at their most removed from the rest of the population. For example, most of the aristocracy spoke French in everyday life, and in the minds of the intelligentsia, a fascination with the heroes of the French Revolution and the ideas of the Enlightenment easily coexisted with the religious tenets of Orthodox Christianity. Meanwhile, Ukraine was divided into several provinces, and its administrative and cultural agency was drastically reduced.

Despite this, Ukraine was able to preserve its identity, and its national cultural canon was gradually formed. At first, this happened faster in the field of literature. In 1798, the first three parts of the most momentous work of the era – Ivan

page 134
Taras Shevchenko
Kateryna, 1842
See Fig. 3, p. 142

Kotliarevskyi's burlesque, mock-heroic poem *Eneida* – were published. This was the first work ever written in colloquial Ukrainian: it formed the basis for both the development of the literary Ukrainian language, and of a new national literature. At the same time, the visual arts were evolving. In the early nineteenth century, they were dominated by such traditional genres as portrait and landscape painting, while the development of sacred art somewhat slowed down, when compared to previous eras. At the very beginning of the century, Ukrainian portraiture still showed the influence of Cossack-era art, with its devotion to flatness and ornateness. Gradually, under the influence of the Imperial Academy of Arts, founded in St Petersburg in 1757, painting techniques improved. The Academy served as a guide for Ukrainian artists of the Russian Empire for a long time – Ukraine did not have its own fine art educational institutions until the end of the nineteenth century.

During this period, portrait painting was especially quick to advance. This was due primarily to demand – the main customers of portraits were rich aristocrats. There were only a few years left before the invention of photography, and oil painting techniques had reached such a level of accessibility that even those of average income could afford to preserve their image and that of their loved ones for eternity in a realistic and high-quality portrait.

At a time when Ukraine was, politically, at its most integrated into the imperial Russian administration, there was a surge of interest in Cossack heritage, Ukrainian folklore, and the Ukraine of old. This was linked to the spread of Romanticism more widely in Europe and the movement's focus on questions of national identity. Between 1827 and 1849, the folklorist Mykhailo Maksymovych published three volumes of a collection of Ukrainian folk songs, which had an enormous impact. In Galicia (the region spanning present-day southeastern Poland and western Ukraine, then under the rule of the Austro-Hungarian Empire), the literary group Ruska Triitsia (Ruthenian Triad) was formed. Its members were influenced by Romanticism and the works of artists from eastern Ukraine. The group travelled around Galicia and Carpathian Ruthenia, recorded folklore, wrote a collection of poetry called *Syn Rusi* (The Son of Rus), and published the almanac *Rusalka Dnistrovaia* (The Dnister Nymph, 1836).

In Ukrainian lands that were part of the Russian Empire, art and culture existed under strict censorship in the second half of the nineteenth century. Because of this, the popular genre of historical painting developed much less actively in Ukrainian territories than in Russian ones. In 1863, the Valuev Circular was published. This decree forbade the printing of religious and educational literature in Ukrainian; only works that were considered 'fine literature' were allowed. In 1876, the even-harsher Ems Ukaz was issued, which essentially banned the Ukrainian language in the Russian Empire and the import of Ukrainian books from abroad. Exceptions were made for historical documents and 'belles lettres', though with stipulations and remaining subject to censorship. Ukrainian theatre, performances of Ukrainian songs, and teaching Ukrainian in elementary schools were all prohibited. Some of these restrictions were lifted in the early 1880s, but the general goal of suppressing the Ukrainian national movement and erasing its collective memory held strong. The Ems Ukaz was lifted only after 1905.

In the second half of the nineteenth century, the Wanderers (Peredvizhniki) played a prominent role in the arts in Ukraine. This group of artists were looking for a way out of what they saw as a crisis of academic art. Inspired by the politically radical notions held by educated circles of society, and in particular, by their enthusiasm for populism, the Wanderers rejected elitism and emphasized enlightenment. The peak of the Wanderers' activity was in the 1870s and 1880s. Their paintings were an experiment in adapting a conservative visual style to the social agenda of the approaching new century, with its forthcoming proletarian revolution. By the end of the nineteenth century, however, this idea of compromising between old form and new content was exhausted, and the art of the Wanderers stagnated.

Russia was the centre of the Wanderers' movement, but notable contributions were made by a number of artists from Ukraine. Mykola Kuznetsov, hailing from Odesa, became an important representative; Porfyrii Martynovych from Kharkiv also exhibited with artists in the group; and Kyriak Kostandi, an outstanding representative of the Odesa school, was closely associated with the movement. Kostandi was not only an artist but a pedagogue, public figure, and museum director who had a great influence on the development of art in Odesa. In 1890 he became one of the founders of the Society of South Russian Artists. The society was created on the model of the Wanderers and played a key role in the cultural life of the city in the late nineteenth and early twentieth centuries.

Until the end of the nineteenth century, Ukrainian art depended on Russian organizations – in particular, the Imperial Academy of Arts – as well as on European academies, where artists often travelled to study. There were no fully fledged art schools in Ukrainian cities until the late nineteenth and early twentieth centuries. The Grekov Odesa Art School received official status as an art academy in 1899. In Kharkiv in 1869, artist Maria Raievska-Ivanova opened the first private school of drawing and painting in the Russian Empire. In Kyiv, Mykola Murashko's drawing school was the basis for the new Kyiv Art School in 1901. Artists who taught there included Fedir Krychevskyi, Mykola Pymonenko, and Oleksandr Murashko. Among its students were future avant-garde artists including Kazimir Malevich, Oleksandra Ekster, and Oleksandr Arkhypenko. During the short-lived independent Ukrainian People's Republic, the Ukrainian Academy of Art was established on 18 December 1917.

At the end of the nineteenth and start of the twentieth centuries, Kyiv was developing rapidly, turning into a metropolis with great cultural ambitions. This was partly due to the expansion of capitalism in Ukraine and the rapid growth of industry. The Tereshchenko family, Ukraine's largest sugar producers and landowners, had supported the Ukrainian art movement for decades. The father Ivan and son Mykhailo were among the Russian Empire's main art collectors and philanthropists. After the Russian Revolution in 1917, their collection was nationalized and formed the basis of the Kyiv Picture Gallery collection, housed in a mansion first built for Ivan

Tereshchenko's father Mykola. Next door is another mansion turned into a museum – the former home of prominent Kyiv philanthropists Bohdan and Varvara Khanenko (Mykola Tereshchenko's eldest daughter), where their collection of classical European and Asian art is still exhibited. In 1899 in Kyiv, in a building built by the famous fin-de-siècle Polish architect Władysław Horodecki, the City Museum of Antiques and Arts was opened. Half of the funds for the construction of the museum were provided by the Tereshchenko family. Today, the museum is called the National Art Museum of Ukraine (NAMU) and holds the world's most representative collection of Ukrainian art. Horodecki also constructed the ornate House with Chimaeras (pictured above), now an official presidential residence.

At the beginning of the twentieth century, Ukrainian art was at a crossroads. Across the world, the crisis facing academic art, the inability of the realist painting tradition to respond to the invention of photography, and the demands of a growing capitalist society, all led to the rapid development of a global form of Modernism. It was this movement that would come to define several generations of artists. The year 1917 was approaching and a general sense of social catastrophe and transformation hung in the air. In artists' studios, a revolution was already in full swing. In just fifteen years, there had been a swift metamorphosis from the colonial Romanticism and ethnographic realism of Mykola Pymonenko: it began with timid experiments in Impressionism, then a surge of interest in Modernism, the cosmopolitan avant-garde, and finally, a focus on utopian non-objective art. This was a period of radical reorientation for Ukrainian art, as it moved from the local to having a pan-European reach, to becoming integrated into a global movement. A mix of Modernist tendencies, characteristic of European art at the end of the nineteenth and beginning of the twentieth centuries, became reference points for artists in both parts of Ukraine – those controlled by the Russian and by the Austro-Hungarian empires. In a sense, this was the most powerful wave of global influences in the history of Ukrainian art. The next time Ukrainian art found itself so in sync with the global art scene was at the end of the twentieth century, with the arrival of the first post-Perestroika generation of artists.

Serfs and Their Masters

In the first half of the nineteenth century, a large part of the Ukrainian population was subject to conditions akin to slavery. Under serfdom, peasants were bound by law to land that was owned by a lord. Serfdom was abolished in the Russian Empire only in 1861. At first glance, during this period there were two completely separate strands of art and culture: the first served the needs of the elite, while the second was considered lowbrow and for the people. In fact, the division between 'high' and popular art was not insuperable. Art for the elites was often created by people born into serfdom, and popular art sometimes borrowed from the aesthetics and technological inventions of fine art.

One of the chief representatives of Ukrainian and Russian imperial art during the late eighteenth and early nineteenth centuries was Volodymyr Borovykovskyi, academician of the Imperial Academy of Arts. Borovykovskyi was a native of Myrhorod, a city in Poltava oblast that was celebrated in the 1830s by Mykola Hohol (also known as Nikolai Gogol), the celebrated Ukrainian–Russian author. Borovykovskyi's family had Ukrainian Cossack roots: his father was the icon painter Luka Borovyk (whose last name means 'Boletus mushroom' in Ukrainian). Old Cossack families often had such amusing surnames, so it is telling that, like many members of the Cossack elite at the time, the Borovyk family 'ennobled' their surname, resulting in the more aristocratic and less typically Ukrainian-sounding name Borovykovskyi. In his youth, Borovykovskyi served in the army, but later devoted himself entirely to painting. He began with icon painting, and after moving to St Petersburg he became a well-known portrait painter, and a master of small-scale and ceremonial portraits.

Part of Borovykovskyi's great legacy is the impressive portrait of Dmytro Troshchynskyi (Fig. 1), a distinguished imperial figure of the late eighteenth to early nineteenth centuries and a powerful landowner from an old Ukrainian Cossack family. The portrait is made in the style of a ceremonial portrait, typical of the era. The fact that the painting depicts a major statesman is indicated by the orders on his shoulder, and the subject's very haughty expression. Troshchynskyi is depicted against a background of art objects, which is clearly a reference to his role as a patron and connoisseur of fine arts. Troshchynskyi held key positions in the Russian Empire – he was Minister of Allotments, then Minister of Justice – but toward the end of his life, he retired to his native Poltava oblast. There, he owned six thousand peasants and a huge estate with the village of Kybyntsi at its centre. Locals called Kybyntsi the 'Ukrainian Athens' because of the proliferation of cultural life at Troshchynskyi's estate: artists came here by invitation; it was the site of Troshchynskyi's famous home theatre, which used serfs of the magnate as actors; and the most prominent aristocrats and leading intellectuals of the era came to visit.

1
Volodymyr Borovykovskyi
Portrait of the Minister of Justice Dmytro Prokopovych Troshchynskyi, 1819
Oil on canvas
100 × 83 cm
National Art Museum
of Ukraine, Kyiv

The existence of serf artists in this era blurred the line between aristocratic and folk art. Aristocrats often taught talented young men from among their peasants the basics of fine art, subsequently using their practically free labour to have portraits made and to decorate their luxurious estates. One of the most prominent serf artists of the early nineteenth century was the Russian Vasily Tropinin. Born in captivity, he briefly studied at the Imperial Academy of Arts, but was then called to join his landowner at his estate in the village of Kukavka in west-central Ukraine. Tropinin spent almost twenty years there, carrying out his duties as an artist, architect, and drawing teacher for landlords' children. It was in Kukavka that he created a panorama of portraits of Ukrainian residents of various social classes (Fig. 2). In his art, Tropinin paid great attention to his brothers in serfdom – the Ukrainian peasants. Today, his realistic paintings make it possible to reconstruct the appearance of Ukrainians in the early nineteenth century. At the age of forty-seven, Tropinin was granted freedom for his outstanding work, though his children remained serfs.

2 (*below left*)
Vasily Tropinin
Ukrainian Man, 1820
Oil on canvas
65.5 × 49.5 cm
National Art Museum
of Ukraine, Kyiv

3 (*below right*)
Taras Shevchenko
Kateryna, 1842
Oil on canvas
93 × 72.3 cm
National Museum of
Taras Shevchenko, Kyiv

The most significant individual to bridge the gap between elite and peasant art was also the most important poet and artist in the history of Ukraine: Taras Shevchenko (1814–61). Shevchenko is not merely a cultural figure for Ukraine. He is a symbol – an icon – for whom there is no equal in the history of the country. Shevchenko was born into a family of serfs, and his parents died early. He showed extraordinary artistic abilities from an early age and learnt drawing from a rural church clerk and painters. At the age of sixteen, he became a servant of the landowner Pavel Engelhardt, with whom he moved to St Petersburg in 1831. There, he studied drawing with Vasily Shiriaev, a little-known guild artist. In 1836, Shevchenko met a fellow countryman, the Ukrainian artist Ivan Soshenko, who, in turn, introduced him to the famous Russian artists Alexei Venetsianov and Karl Briullov, as well as the poet Vasily Zhukovsky. Struck by the young serf's talents, the artists were able to buy his freedom from Engelhardt – though with great difficulty. Taras Shevchenko was then accepted into the Imperial Academy of Arts, becoming a student of Karl Briullov.

As well as drawing and painting, Shevchenko wrote poetry. In 1840, a small collection of his poems was published, titled *Kobzar* (The Bard). This book would become a turning point in the history of Ukrainian literature and culture. Across the country, its pages were worn thin with use and its words learnt by heart, both in the salons of the intelligentsia and in poor, rural homes. As an artist, Shevchenko was of course talented, especially in graphic arts. But as a poet, he was a genius. In 1842 Shevchenko created his most significant painting, *Kateryna*. The painting is based on one of Shevchenko's own poems, in which he recounts the unfortunate fate of a Ukrainian girl of the same name. Having fallen in love with a visiting Russian soldier, Kateryna soon realizes that she is expecting his child, but the cowardly soldier abandons the girl. Kateryna remains alone and faces extreme cruelty and condemnation from society. Both the poem and the painting – for their insight into the tragedy women faced in patriarchal society, and for Shevchenko's courage in choosing such a subject – know no equals in the history of Ukrainian art, or indeed, the art of the Russian Empire of the time.

In 1847 in Kyiv, Shevchenko became close to the historian Mykola Kostomarov and joined the Brotherhood of Saints Cyril and Methodius, a small underground circle of intelligentsia interested in the idea of a democratic union of the Slavic republics, with its centre in Kyiv. Shevchenko was arrested for his participation in this society, but, unlike the rest of its members, he suffered a disproportionately harsh punishment. Taking revenge on the former serf for his strongly worded, nationalist poems that criticized tsarist Russia, the imperial administration sent Shevchenko into exile as a soldier in the Orenburg region. Shevchenko then spent ten years in deserted fortresses on the border of modern-day Russia and Kazakhstan and on the shores of the Aral Sea. The cruelty of the sentence was compounded by an explicit ban on drawing. Despite these setbacks, Shevchenko created some of the most important graphic works in the history of Ukrainian art in exile. In his small, ascetic sketches, he documented the surrounding landscapes, as well as everyday life in soldiers' barracks and Kazakh villages.

Contested Imperial Legacies

Because of Ukraine's colonial position within the Russian Empire, it is difficult to unambiguously categorize most of its nineteenth- and early twentieth-century artists as having either Ukrainian or Russian origins. Most often, such artists had both; they were hybrid figures. What differentiated them was their degree of interest in Ukraine and Ukrainian issues, though often this was simply determined by their place of birth. Many artists who seem at first only nominally connected with Ukraine in fact produced important works and cycles with Ukrainian themes, or writings that demonstrate their complex and ambiguous identities. One example is Ivan Aivazovsky, an outstanding seascape painter of Armenian origin born in Feodosia (Crimea). An important part of his legacy are remarkable works featuring Ukraine, such as *Windmills in the Ukrainian Steppe at Sunset* (1862), *Ukrainian Landscape with Chumaks in the Moonlight* (1869), and *Mill on the Riverbank. Ukraine* (1880). Arkhyp Kuindzhi, an artist of Greek origin originally from Mariupol, also created several works with Ukrainian themes: *Ukrainian Night* (1876), *Evening in Ukraine* (1878), and *The Dnipro in the Morning* (1881). Kuindzhi's masterpiece is the painting *Moonlit Night on the Dnipro* (1880). He repeated the theme of this famous work in another painting: *Night on the Don* (1882; Fig. 4), today part of the Kyiv Picture Gallery collection.

Marie Bashkirtseff was one of the few women among a predominantly male sphere of artists in the nineteenth century. Bashkirtseff is known around the world as a Russian artist, although she was born and lived in Poltava oblast in Ukraine until she was twelve years old. Later, Bashkirtseff left for western Europe, where she studied painting and kept a diary. It was this diary that brought her posthumous fame: Bashkirtseff died of tuberculosis when she was just twenty-five years old. The Dnipro Art Museum houses the painting *In the Studio* (1881; Fig. 5, p. 146), created by Bashkirtseff at the age of twenty-three. The work shows a life-painting lesson in Paris in the late nineteenth century, and demonstrates how many women of this period had a very keen interest in art classes.

Many Russian artists spent time working in Ukraine during various periods and influenced the development of local art. The Ukrainian context is just as

4
Arkhyp Kuindzhi
***Night on the Don**,* 1882
Oil on canvas
Kyiv Picture Gallery

'Many artists who seem at first only nominally connected with Ukraine have in fact produced important works and cycles with Ukrainian themes, or writings that demonstrate their complex and ambiguous identities.'

'Bashkirtseff is known around the world as a Russian
artist, although she was born and lived in Poltava
oblast in Ukraine until she was twelve years old.'

5 (*opposite*)
Marie Bashkirtseff
In the Studio, **1881**
Oil on canvas
154 × 188 cm
Dnipro Art Museum

6
St Volodymyr's Cathedral
(interior)
1862–82
Kyiv

important for understanding the work of these artists themselves. For example, in the mid-1880s, Mikhail Vrubel – the most important representative of Russian Modernism and symbolism – worked in Kyiv. There, he painted frescoes and icons for St Cyril's Monastery and sketched frescoes for St Volodymyr's Cathedral. He also began to develop the pivotal motif often repeated in his work, the demon. Vrubel's Kyiv period (as well his more mature works) would later have a significant influence on the development of Modernism in Ukraine. Another representative of Art Nouveau, the Polish painter Wilhelm Kotarbiński, lived and worked in Kyiv from the 1880s until his death in 1921. Under the leadership of Viktor Vasnetsov, he was also involved in painting the frescoes at St Volodymyr's Cathedral.

The decoration of the interior of St Volodymyr's Cathedral was a milestone in the development of Kyiv's artistic life at the end of the nineteenth century. The project was overseen by Adrian Prakhov, a leading St Petersburg professor, art historian, and archaeologist. His role in the progress of art of later years is difficult to overestimate. It was he who invited famous Russian artists to come to Kyiv to work on the cathedral: Viktor Vasnetsov, Mikhail Nesterov, the brothers Pavel and Alexander Svedomsky, as well as Vrubel and Kotarbiński.

National Identity

Modernism made its way into Ukrainian art quite gradually. It coincided with the search for new political ideas and the awakening of a national consciousness. At the end of the nineteenth century, despite the division of Ukraine under the rule of two empires, interest in its history was growing. The foundation was being laid for understanding Ukraine as an autonomous cultural and historical entity. In this context, paintings with folkloric and historical themes were of especially great importance, and these works played a significant role in shaping the identity of the new Ukrainian intelligentsia. At the beginning of the twentieth century, artistic expression would undergo radical changes; however, the search for a national style can be seen across the works of artists with completely different views and backgrounds.

An important figure for understanding the subsequent development of Ukrainian art is Ilya Repin, one of the best painters of the late nineteenth century. A native of Chuhuiv in Kharkiv oblast, Repin was educated in St Petersburg and later became an active member of the Wanderers. Although Repin was a prominent

7
Ilya Repin
Reply of the Zaporizhian Cossacks, 1893 (second version)
Oil on canvas
174 × 265 cm
Kharkiv Art Museum

Mykola Pymonenko
Stop Fooling Around, 1895
Oil on canvas
79 × 108 cm
National Art Museum
of Ukraine, Kyiv

representative of the imperial artistic establishment, throughout his life he retained
an interest in his homeland and its history, socialized with Ukrainian cultural figures,
and devoted a number of works to Ukrainian subjects. The most famous of these
is *Reply of the Zaporizhian Cossacks* (1880–91). The creation of this large-scale
historical painting was inspired by Repin's conversations with Dmytro Yavornytskyi,
a leading historian of the Zaporizhian Cossacks, and his own expedition in 1880 to
territories previously occupied by the Zaporizhian Sich. Repin's work has become
one of the most iconic paintings on the subject of Ukraine. It influenced the
formation of Ukrainian historical painting, the development of the image of the
Zaporizhian Cossacks in popular culture, and has even indirectly affected the
aesthetics of protests in contemporary, independent Ukraine. In the twentieth
century, Repin would inspire not only renowned socialist realists, but also the
leaders of Kyiv's unofficial intellectual society of the 1960s and 70s.

Another realist of the late nineteenth to early twentieth century, whose work
significantly influenced the formation of the Ukrainian school of painting, was the
Wanderer Mykola Pymonenko. His work featured numerous snippets of folk life, an
abundance of ethnographic details, sentimentality, and a bright palette. Pymonenko
painted a romanticized image of the Ukrainian village, perfectly reflecting the
stereotypical view of 'Little Russia's' local charm held by the Russian Empire. The
fate of the painting *Stop Fooling Around* (1895) is an interesting one. The painting shows
an angry mother heading toward two lovers, who are unceremoniously embracing,
against the backdrop of a Ukrainian pastoral landscape. As art became increasingly
reproduced on a mass scale, this ironic vignette of peasant life would become a 'cult
classic'. Thousands of reproductions and different versions were sold and gave rise to
one of the most popular images of twentieth-century Ukrainian folk painting. Among
researchers, this popular folk image has been referred to as 'Petro and Natalia, run!

Mama's coming with a rolling pin' – according to the distinctive inscription seen on many paintings of this type. With the advent of mass distribution of reproductions at the beginning of the twentieth century, the crossover of narratives from paintings by eminent artists into folk art became ubiquitous.

In the work of Kharkiv resident Serhii Vasylkivskyi, there is a consistent interest in Ukrainian antiquity. Vasylkivskyi was very prolific, and left behind several thousand artworks, largely dominated by steppe landscapes, historical sketches, and scenes

from the life of Ukrainian Cossacks and peasants. The painting *The Chumak Road to Romodan* depicts Chumaks, Ukrainian merchants who engaged in trade and transportation of goods along the so-called Chumatsky Way. Along this route, merchants carried salt to southern and central Ukraine from the Black Sea coast of Crimea, and sent bread and other agricultural goods back. The great importance of this transport artery in Ukrainian culture and folklore is eloquently reflected by the fact that in the Ukrainian language, the Milky Way galaxy is called the Chumatsky Way.

9
Serhii Vasylkivskyi
The Chumak Road to Romodan,
1910s
Oil on canvas
60 × 106 cm
National Art Museum
of Ukraine, Kyiv

Folk Art

While the fine art of palaces seemed far removed from the art of peasants, the two did subtly intersect. As Romanticism grew, so did the influence of folk culture on the art of the elite. Similarly, the resonance of aristocratic culture was often seen in folk art. One example is the genealogy of western Ukrainian ceramic tiles, which many researchers note can be traced back to similar products made for noble estates of the period (see pp. 106–7).

An important technique for the rapid, pre-industrial mass production of art objects came to western Ukraine from central and western Europe in the middle of the nineteenth century. This novel technique – in which painted images were applied to the reverse of glass – instantly gained popularity due to its expressive ornateness and depth of colour (Fig. 10). The glass, to which the drawing was applied, simultaneously served as a protective cover for the work. In western Ukraine, the technique of reverse glass painting was especially in demand for the manufacture of icons for the home. Gradually, Galicia developed its own art style, distinct from other regional styles, such as the Romanian. There, icon painting on glass also became widespread.

An image that is nearly universal in Ukrainian art is that of the Cossack Mamai. The image has an elegiac tone: a Cossack sits cross-legged and plays the bandura, a traditional musical instrument; his simple belongings are nearby; a horse grazes in the distance. About whom does the lonely Ukrainian warrior compose his song?

10 (*left and far left*)
Traditional Volyn glass paintings,
19th century
Ostroh, Rivne oblast

11 (*opposite*)
Unknown artist
Cossack Bandura Player,
First half of 19th century
Oil on canvas
National Art Museum
of Ukraine, Kyiv

Is it for his lost comrades, about a world that is far from perfect, or about his lost fate? The genealogy of this story is rooted in ancient times. Some researchers have even noted similarities between Mamai and traditional Buddhist icons, which were a fairly common decorative element in the dwellings of medieval nomads in the Eurasian Steppe. The region of Ukraine in which the Mamai image spread overlapped with the borders of the Hetmanate, which indicates the hereditary connection of this image, first and foremost, with the memory of the Cossacks. One way or another, in the nineteenth century, the Cossack Mamai could be found in almost every Ukrainian home – whether a rural hut or a lord's luxurious estate.

The Dawn of Modernism

Ukrainian Art Nouveau artists reflect a bright kaleidoscope of personalities and stories. Perhaps the most important Ukrainian painter of the early twentieth century was the Kyiv native Oleksandr Murashko. Murashko was a graduate of the Imperial Academy of Arts, a student of Ilya Repin, a member of the Munich Secession (the group of artists who broke from the mainstream Munich Artists' Association in 1892), and a frequent visitor to Paris. He was well acquainted with Impressionism and developed his own style, in which he combined the Secession's typical palette and Parisian lightness and elegance with Ukrainian hallmarks. Murashko was especially successful in portraiture. In his paintings, he paid particular attention to the use of colour to depict light and shadow. It was this dazzling play of highlights and splashes of colour that hypnotized viewers and became the focus of most of his later works. In 1909, Murashko's painting *Carousel*, depicting two young girls at a lively folk fair, received a medal at an exhibition in Munich. It is now in the collection of the Museum of Fine Arts in Budapest. In 1910, two of Murashko's works were exhibited at the Venice Biennale, and in 1911 to 1912 he took part in several Munich Secession exhibitions. *Annunciation* is one of Murashko's most famous paintings. The artist was inspired by a domestic scene in his house: he saw a young girl open a light tulle curtain and enter from the terrace. Murashko was captivated by the magic of the moment and thought that the Archangel Gabriel must have entered the chambers of Mary in just the same way – easily and noiselessly – to bring her the Good News.

At the beginning of the twentieth century, Poltava native Vsevolod Maksymovych came onto the scene: his art was shaped not only by Gustav Klimt and Aubrey Beardsley, but also by the paintings of Mikhail Vrubel and Russian symbolism. The artist was a bright but short-lived spark on the horizon of Ukrainian Art Nouveau. At the age of twenty, he committed suicide. Nevertheless, in just two years – from 1912 to 1914 – Maksymovych managed to produce an impressive number of paintings; make friends with artists in Moscow such as the poet Velimir Khlebnikov, painter Mikhail Larionov, poet Vasily Kamensky, and other Futurists; star in the lost avant-garde film *Drama in the Futurists' Cabaret* (1914); and reinterpret the Vienna Secession

12
Oleksandr Murashko
Annunciation, 1909
Oil on canvas
198 × 169 cm
National Art Museum
of Ukraine, Kyiv

'In his paintings, [Murashko] paid particular attention to the use of colour to depict light and shadow. It was this dazzling play of highlights and splashes of colour that hypnotized viewers and became the focus of most of his later works.'

movement through the prism of ancient aesthetics. In Maksymovych's works, ornamental scenes of sumptuous feasts (Fig. 13), references to ancient stories, the cult of beautiful bodies, decadence, and erotica were woven into a spectacular medley, attesting to the young artist's extraordinary talent.

The Vienna Secession (like in Munich, formed by a group of artists who resigned from the official art association in 1897) was a fertile source of inspiration for Ukrainian artists at the beginning of the twentieth century. The main representative of this current of the Ukrainian Art Nouveau was the artist, poet, and playwright Mykhailo Zhuk. Zhuk brought the fashionable Secession style to Ukraine from the Academy of Fine Arts in Kraków, where he studied under the famous Polish Modernist Stanisław Wyspiański. Zhuk is also inextricably linked with Odesa, where he lived for many years, notably as prorector of the Odesa Art Institute, which soon became the Odesa Art School. Even before the Russian Revolution in 1917, Zhuk taught drawing to the Ukrainian poet Pavlo Tychyna at the Chernihiv seminary. The two talented men's similar worldviews marked the beginning of a friendship. Tychyna became the main subject in Zhuk's three-panel mural *White and Black* (1912–14). The young Modernist poet – whose literary works from this period provide no hint of his future as a major Soviet writer and vocal supporter of collectivization and Stalinist industrialization – appears in the form of a dark angel. The mural combines plant motifs (typical for Zhuk), symbolist poetry, and rich ornateness characteristic of the Secession movement.

13
Vsevolod Maksymovych
Banquet, 1913
Oil on canvas
210 × 335 cm
National Art Museum
of Ukraine, Kyiv

The dark angel plays the flute, and a teenage girl with white wings listens to him, frozen either in prayer or in shy uncertainty. Or perhaps she senses the coming transformation of the poet-werewolf Tychyna and the sad fate of the staggeringly beautiful Ukrainian land that extends behind the wings of the figures in the painting.

In western Ukraine, then under the rule of Austria–Hungary, Modernism developed in a different cultural context and was heavily influenced by Polish, Austrian, and Hungarian art of the epoch. However, several artists encompass both Ukrainian contexts, as if anticipating the future of a unified Ukrainian art. An important figure for understanding the progression of the western Ukrainian artistic tradition is Oleksa Novakivskyi, a graduate of the Academy of Fine Arts in Kraków who worked at the intersection of Impressionism, Post-Impressionism and Expressionism. Novakivskyi moved to Lviv in 1913 at the invitation of a prominent patron of the arts and founder of the National Museum of Lviv, Metropolitan Andrei Sheptytskyi. Sheptytskyi's role in the development of Ukrainian art in the first decades of the twentieth century is difficult to overestimate. The philanthropist was open-minded for a metropolitan (an Orthodox and Greek Catholic religious title, similar to a cardinal in Roman Catholicism) and supported the Modernist art movement. Because of his authority, Modernism in Lviv was bound up with religious themes.

In 1923, with the support of Sheptytskyi, Novakivskyi founded an art school in Lviv. It was attended by many key artists of subsequent movements, such as Roman Selskyi. In Novakivskyi's work, Modernist techniques are closely intertwined with Ukrainian traditions and religious aesthetics. The mythological image of Leda, the mother of Helen of Troy, whom the almighty Zeus seduced in the guise of a swan, is also a recurring motif in Novakivskyi's work (Fig. 15, pp. 158–59). Novakivskyi created several works at the same time that play on this eternal love story of a deity and an earthly woman.

15
Oleksa Novakivskyi
Leda, 1920s
Charcoal on paper
143 × 220 cm
Private collection

Kabat
1920
Sian region, western Ukraine
Homemade linen; sewing machine,
linen weaving
Length 51 cm

Women's outerwear
1883
Middle Dnipro, Kyiv region,
north-central Ukraine
Homemade cloth; felting, hand
sewing, appliqué, machine tailoring,
hand embroidery
Length 103 cm

Children's shirt
20th century
Hutsul region, western Ukraine
Cotton fabric, satin, factory fabric;
hand sewing, stem seam, hand
embroidery
Length 43 cm

Historically, Ukrainian costume combined characteristic
Slavic decorations and elements of design that came
to Ukraine from the Eurasian steppe. See page 242.

Children's waistcoat
20th century
Pokuttia region, southwestern
Ukraine
Sewing machine, factory weaving
Length 28 cm

Manta wedding dress
Early 20th century
Hutsul region, western Ukraine
Homemade cloth; felting, hand
sewing, hand embroidery, weaving
Length 117 cm

Women's shirt
1876
Podillia region, western Ukraine
Hand sewing and embroidery
Length 57 cm

AVANT-GARDE
ART & THEATRE

1890 to 1939

Myroslava M. Mudrak

I n the short span of only half a century, Ukrainian modern art experienced an unexpected and abrupt birth that established new front lines in global visual culture. Ukraine's territory served as a cradle of nascent Modernism, which sprung up organically from local initiatives. At the dawn of the twentieth century, only the imposing post-Impressionist canvases of the French-influenced Oleksandr Murashko ('Ukraine's Manet'), the landscapes of academically trained Mykola Pymonenko (the first teacher of Kazimir Malevich, who would become the originator of Suprematism), and the intimate realist scenes of Odesa's skilled artists with populist sympathies, characterized the contemporary Ukrainian artistic scene. Albeit a celebrated chapter in Ukraine's history of Modernism, its amorphous nature was quickly overshadowed by a new generation bent on more radical approaches.

As early as 1908, the adventurous, gregarious, and highly enterprising Davyd Burliuk, proud of his Cossack heritage, organized the 'Lanka' ('Link') exhibition in Kyiv – a brash stand against vernacular tastes. In his opening statement, Burliuk defended the innately autonomous nature of painting that he believed would extricate it from long-held traditions of description, illusion, and narrative content. Burliuk promoted the abandonment of all qualities of 'literariness' in visual representation, in favour of a fiery 'New Art' that would be self-generating, like a 'flaming column, carrying the soul'. In 1909, together with his sculptor friend Volodymyr Izdebskyi, Burliuk organized a touring exhibition of French masters, which was launched in Odesa. The so-called Izdebskyi International Salon travelled on to Kyiv, then to St Petersburg and Riga. Along its way it galvanized a younger generation of aspiring artists to understand and approach artmaking with a new vision. A second salon followed in 1910. This time, it included locally grown painters: Wassily Kandinsky from Odesa; Volodymyr Tatlin, and the Burliuk brothers, Davyd and Volodymyr from the Kharkiv and Kherson oblasts; as well as Oleksandra Ekster from Kyiv.

In 1914, Kyiv held its first independent modern art exhibition, 'Kiltse' ('Ring'), which brought into prominence the unique talent of Ekster and Oleksandr Bohomazov – both firebrands of Ukrainian Modernism. Committed to introducing modernity to Ukrainian visual culture and poised to move in step with developments in the West, they sought to liberate art from tired conventions of mimetic representation and instead to treat the art object as a direct expression of modernity. Painterly elements – line, colour, volume, space, and rhythm, coordinated into a composition within a picture space and on a picture surface – constituted the language of art and was the sole required vehicle for relaying experience in the modern world. Through the end of the 1910s, experimentation with the potential of pictorial language surfaced in artistic hubs throughout Ukraine and defined the avant-garde of Kyiv, Kharkiv, and Odesa. Ukraine was abuzz with pockets of activity among mostly self-trained artists who had minimal exposure to formal art schooling,

page 162
Vadym Meller
Sketch of choreographic
movement 'Masks', 1919
See Fig. 5, p. 174

yet they set new directions for the future. In addition to joining in with progressive artists across Europe in establishing an influential front line for the visual arts, the primary feature of Ukraine's avant-garde was its intimate connection to a native, if not national, worldview.

Prior to that, artistic life in Ukraine under imperial Russia endured a forced homogeneous culture that paid no heed to national origins. Although private studios and small art schools could be found in Ukraine from the 1890s onward, aspiring artists often made their way to Paris or Munich. They found friendly support among émigrés at Marie Vassilieff's Académie Russe or at schools such as the Académie Ranson in Paris. World-famous Oleksandr Arkhypenko established himself as early as 1908 in Paris, actively exhibiting together with the leading artists of Modernism and opening his own school in 1912 (see Fig. 11, p. 180). Artists from western Ukraine such as Mykhailo Boichuk trained in Kraków and then went further west to the art capitals of Europe, where Boichuk caught the attention of French critics. The outbreak of the First World War and the Bolshevik Revolution in Russia interrupted these pursuits, and many such artists returned to Ukraine to find their place in a sovereign state.

An intermingling of ethnicities on Ukraine's territories contributed further to the unique nature of Modernism in Ukraine. The local chapter of the Jewish Kultur Lige explored Cubo-Futurist principles while promoting Yiddish culture in Kyiv and Odesa. Artists Issakhar-Ber Rybak, El (Lazar) Lissitzky, and Mark Epstein (see p. 166) found creative spaces in Ukraine. Russian Futurist poets were co-opted into the circle of Kharkiv's Soiuz Semy (Union of Seven), headed by Borys Kosarev, an entrepreneurial artist gifted with diverse talents, from graphics and painting to theatre. The bawdy art of Davyd Burliuk and his association with Russian Futurist poets gained him the moniker of the 'Father of Russian Futurism'.

A distinctly Ukrainian Futurism came into being, led by the poet Mykhailo Semenko, who blurred the borders between word and image to create a new hybrid genre he called 'poezo-painting'. By the 1920s, Semenko's ideas had evolved into the concept of Panfuturism, an all-inclusive global view of art, poetry, and literature, including such new genres as photography, cinematography, and photomontage. Adopting the precepts of Constructivism as a system for ordering culture, Semenko's followers, the Panfuturists, operated on the principle of a cross-fertilization of artistic ideas by highlighting Ukraine's own cutting-edge scene: a synthesis of early twentieth-century movements such as Dadaism, Cubism, and Futurism, at a new Panfuturist stage of modernity. They demonstrated this stance in their Kharkiv journal, *Nova Heneratsiia* (New Generation), published from 1927 to 1930.

Before 1917, the pursuit of a Ukrainian profile in Modernist art could only be a matter of the heart and a strong desire to see Ukrainian artistic production as separate from Russian, grounded in reasons of geography, history, and tradition.

At the proclamation of independence after the Russian Revolution, the founding of the Ukrainian Academy of Art in 1917 set forth new orientations in art with the support of the new republican government. Basing its curriculum on specialized workshops headed by accomplished Modernists, not unlike the model adopted at the Bauhaus in Weimar in 1919, the Academy produced a plethora of artists who carried the banner of Ukrainian Modernism into the tumultuous 1920s. Here, the major Futurist painter Viktor Palmov laid out his colour studies based on the Ostwald system; the architect Vasyl Krychevskyi and his brother Fedir taught the principles of modern painting; Heorhii Narbut headed the graphics division; and Mykhailo Boichuk created a school of monumental painting. Although Ukrainian independence was short-lived, modern artistic culture took hold because of the engagement of the avant-garde.

After the regime change that followed the Bolshevik takeover, the Academy had taken on a productionist role, and in 1924 it was renamed the Kyiv Art Institute. Under the Bolsheviks, from 1919 to 1934, Kharkiv was the capital of Soviet Ukraine. As the seat of Ukrainian Constructivism, the city is known as the crucible of twentieth-century industrial production and design. A burgeoning metropolis of factories and manufacturing not only inspired the engineering mind of Volodymyr Tatlin, but was also the site of a prime paradigm of Constructivist architecture: the Derzhprom, known as the Palace of Industry, and a candidate for a pending UNESCO World Heritage Site designation.

By 1927, a decade after the Bolshevik Revolution, Ukrainian art had largely discovered its own identity thanks in part to a government-sponsored 'indigenization' programme. From 1923 until the Stalinist purges in the 1930s, the policy of Ukrainianization brought about a true national cultural rebirth, while at the same time identifying the key personnages of Ukraine's cultural elite. One of the most ambitious was theatre director Les Kurbas. His brainchild, the artistic union Berezil, represented a collective of youthful actors, playwrights, and designers who embraced Expressionism and Constructivism to create a theatre of maximum emotional impact through a minimalist stage presentation. Much of the theatre's visual imprint was defined by the award-winning sets and costumes designed by Vadym Meller. Berezil's work was singled out at the 1925 International Exhibition of Modern Decorative and Industrial Arts in Paris. There, Meller's maquette for Berezil's production of the play *Secretary of the Labour Union* was awarded a gold medal, though the honour went to the USSR, not to Ukraine. A repeat of these circumstances took place at the Venice Biennales of 1928 and 1930, when Ukrainian painters Viktor Palmov and Anatol Petrytskyi, as well as Oleksandr Bohomazov, caught the attention of many visitors who were unaware of the Ukrainian origin of these artists.

What has come to be called the Ukrainian avant-garde spanned two tumultuous decades of the early twentieth century: a period accented by a world war, a revolution, the collapse of an empire, and, most importantly, a declaration of national identity, which came to an end through the execution of an entire cultural vanguard. The avant-garde appeared on the scene as abruptly as it was cut short, as the euphoric decade of the 1920s ended. Kurbas, Semenko, Boichuk, and his trusted followers Ivan Padalka and Vasyl Sedliar were all executed in 1937, as waves of Stalinist purges began to diminish the ranks of these artists, bringing the Ukrainian avant-garde to a crushing end.

Mark Epstein
The Cellist, Cubist Composition, c. 1919
Ink and sepia colour aquarelle on paper
41 × 27 cm
National Art Museum of Ukraine, Kyiv

Graphic Arts, Industrial Design, and Architecture

The Poltava Zemstvo (1903–7), designed by Vasyl Krychevskyi, embodies the economy of Modernist design by using subtle variations of colour and organizing the exterior with architectonic simplicity. The exterior of the brick structure is accented with geometric motifs inspired by familiar patterns from local woodcarving and peasant embroidery. Rendered symbolically rather than treated as pure adornment, Krychevskyi's structure embodies a synthesis of the nation's material culture with the utilitarian purpose of modern architecture: the surface is embellished with a band of heraldic shields representing various localities governed by the administrative mandate of the Zemstvo building. The interior of the Poltava Zemstvo, today the city's Museum of Natural History and Culture, is covered with simplified regional designs emulating the familiar floral motifs seen on the whitewashed and painted surfaces of Ukrainian peasant homes. Far from being purely decorative, the holistic plan for the modern building, as envisioned by Krychevskyi, constitutes what came to be known as the Ukrainian Modern style.

This sense of 'owning' modernity in the name of Ukraine comes across in the designs of Heorhii Narbut, who before the Russian Revolution of 1917 was a central player in St Petersburg's art circles, particularly the progressive group called Mir Iskusstva (The World of Art). Pure aestheticism was a primary goal for this association, whose artists gained renown as book illustrators and theatre designers. Their cosmopolitan worldview was matched by a strong wave of rising neo-nationalism and the idea of a mythical revival of Russia's past. Within that milieu, Narbut came to be recognized as one of the leading illustrators of Russian children's books, with a style that emulated the myth-making historicism of illustrator and one-time ethnographer, Ivan Bilibin. The pronouncement of Ukraine's independence after the downfall of the tsars, however, prompted Narbut to return to his homeland, where he became the director of the newly formed Ukrainian Academy of Art in Kyiv and headed the graphics division. Narbut's keen design eye launched a new vision for modern Ukrainian graphics.

1
Poltava Zemstvo
(Poltava Regional Administration Building), 1903–7
Vasyl Krychevskyi (architect)
Poltava

'The interior of the Poltava Zemstvo [...] is covered with simplified regional designs emulating the familiar floral motifs seen on the whitewashed and painted surfaces of Ukrainian peasant homes.'

Narbut created a visual brand for the new, modern Ukrainian polity – a style based on melding the script of Old Slavonic manuscripts of the Kyivan Rus period with the simplified palette and architectonic features of the uniquely Ukrainian Cossack Baroque style. Blending classical Western elements with Ukrainian motifs in his covers for *Mystetstvo* ('Art'), the first magazine in the modern state of Ukraine devoted to art, Narbut introduced a uniquely Ukrainian spirit into modern typographic design. The covers had a fresh imagery that, though Ukrainian in content, was confluent with the new proletarian regime imposed on Ukraine in 1919. Narbut schooled not only an immediate generation of followers who learned to emulate the hallmarks of his style, based on the indigenous Cossack Baroque qualities of the Mazepa era, but also generations of graphic artists that followed and who modelled their logotypes, vignettes, and cover designs for books and magazines on the recognizable features of Narbut's signature style.

No less innovative was Kharkiv-born Vasyl Yermylov, whose industrial reliefs, magazine cover designs, publicly accessible wall newspapers, and product labels signalled a distinct Kharkiv-based, Ukrainian Constructivist aesthetic in the 1920s. Balance, clarity, symmetry, interlinked components, and connectivity between various three-dimensional forms provided these products with a utilitarian purpose: an artistic functionalism that reflected a practical engagement with the working class. Responding to the proletarian rhetoric of the era, Yermylov's art expresses the industrial aura of Kharkiv as the technological heart of Ukraine, with its abundant factories and industrial production. At the same time, it reflects the era of Ukrainianization – a government policy that allowed for Ukrainian identity to enter the cultural sphere, as long as it was 'Soviet' in spirit. Employing only the primary colours of Ukrainian folk art, Yermylov's conceptions are harmoniously composed with both natural and manufactured wood pieces. With the wood pieces placed at angles and layered to create spatial differentiation, the simple relief invites a complex

2a (*below, left*)
Heorhii Narbut
Self-portrait with St George, 1917
Paper, wash, gouache
38.5 × 27.5 cm
National Art Museum of Ukraine, Kyiv

2b (*below, centre*)
Heorhii Narbut
Frontispiece design for the art journal *Mystetstvo* ('Art')
No. 1, 1920
Private collection, Kyiv

2c (*below, right*)
Heorhii Narbut
Frontispiece design for *Mystetstvo*, No. 3, 1919
Gouache and pen on paper
25 × 18 cm
Kharkiv Art Museum, Kharkiv

Vasyl Yermylov
Composition Number 3, 1923
Wood, brass, varnish and paint
32 × 43 × 7.5 cm
Museum of Modern Art (MoMA),
New York

4 (*overleaf*)
Derzhprom
(State Industrial Building), 1925–28
Sergei Serafimov, Samuel Kravets
and Mark Felger (architects)
Kharkiv

of visual and material interrelationships – a Constructivist principle of organized
movement that serves as an abstract template for the whole of modern society.

The icon of Ukrainian architectural Constructivism, the sprawling Derzhprom
(State Industrial Building; sometimes referred to as the Palace of Industry), is the
embodiment of the industrial-functionalist aesthetic. Its integrated, multi-level,
organization of exterior and interior space allows for large public gatherings as well
as efficient office space. Built between 1925 and 1928, the Derzhprom remains one
of the quintessential paradigms of utopian Soviet-era construction and a unique
extant model of Modernist administrative architecture in the USSR. As one of the
highest structures of its time in the Soviet Union, built with reinforced concrete,
the Derzhprom can be seen as a precursor to the modern skyscraper.

Experimental Theatre

One of the main sites of the avant-garde's engagement with the public was on the stage, through theatre and ballet. The peripatetic dancer and choreographer Bronislava Nijinska (1891–1972) founded an innovative School of Movement in Kyiv in 1919. The school functioned as a laboratory for exploring abstract rhythms in music through bodily motion. As a precursor to modern dance, the innovative choreography explored by Nijinska laid the groundwork for unprecedented performative art in Kyiv. As both a teacher and a theorist, Nijinska collaborated with Oleksandra Ekster, whose costume designs and sets embodied the idea of rhythmic and dynamic movement in space, bringing her artistic conceptions from

5
Vadym Meller
Sketch of choreographic movement 'Masks'
for the Bronislava Nijinska
School of Movement, Kyiv, 1919
60 × 43 cm
Museum of Theatre, Music
and Cinema of Ukraine, Kyiv

Vadym Meller
Stage design for *Jimmie Higgins*
Texts by Upton Sinclair
Berezil Artistic Association
Dir. Les Kurbas, 1923
Museum of Theatre, Music
and Cinema of Ukraine, Kyiv

visual abstraction to the dance stage. Ekster's protégés and colleagues, Vadym Meller and Anatol Petrytskyi, implemented the model of their mentor to revolutionize the Ukrainian performative space. Petrytskyi had been the costume designer for the famed choreographer Kasian Goleizovsky (1892–1970; a pioneer in Moscow's avant-garde dance world in the 1920s). He transformed the stage presentations of his native Kyiv's Ivan Franko Theatre with bold costumes and lush backdrops that encapsulated the legacy of a medieval Kyivan spirit, and his (mostly agrarian) countrymen's ardent love of nature, including the bawdiness of the vernacular, steeped in Cossack lore – all of which matched the wit and humour of contemporary modern Ukrainian writers such as Ostap Vyshnia (1889–1956). Through explosive colour and varied textures, and using a myriad of appliqué materials in his theatrical conceptions, Petrytskyi achieved a marriage of the visceral and the intellectual in visual form. As he unleashed the grotesque and the primitive, he also revealed a predilection for structured form: a hallmark of the Ukrainian avant-garde of the 1920s.

'One of the main sites of the avant-garde's engagement with the public was on the theatrical and ballet stage.'

7
Anatol Petrytskyi
Stage design for the set
'On Mars' for the production
of Ostap Vyshnia's *Viy*
Ivan Franko Theatre, Kharkiv,
Dir. H. Yura, 1925
Paper, watercolour, gouache,
appliqué
47 × 68 cm
Museum of Theatre, Music
and Cinema of Ukraine, Kyiv

The Avant-Garde

The influential personality and immeasurable talent of Oleksandra Ekster represents a high point in the launching of the Ukrainian avant-garde. Between Kyiv and the artistic axes of Paris–Milan and Moscow–St Petersburg, Ekster's role was that of a courier of Modernism between western Europe, Russian artists, and her colleagues in Ukraine. As she informed current trends in Cubism in France and Futurism in Italy, her efforts led to local experimentation with abstraction. Ekster's colleague and protégé Oleksandr Bohomazov brought an unadulterated Futurism to Kyiv that went beyond what the Italian Futurists were able to accomplish. During the years 1911 to 1916, Bohomazov focused on Kyiv as a bustling hub, exploring his principles of movement and dynamism in visual representation. Be it in painting or in drawing, Bohomazov's energetic treatment of city life signalled the fulfilment of a clearly

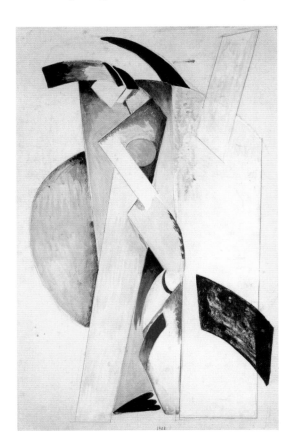

8
Oleksandra Ekster
Composition, 1916
Cardboard, gouache, watercolour, ink
55 × 33.5 cm
Museum of Theatre, Music and Cinema of Ukraine, Kyiv

articulated purpose for the modern artist: to deploy the two-dimensional picture surface as a kind of launchpad for the display of dynamic rhythms and movement confluent with the energy of modern life. Committed to this pursuit, by 1914 Bohomazov had completed a treatise entitled *The Art of Painting and the Elements* in which he laid out the tenets of 'New Art'. Essential to his theoretical position is the idea that only diagonals and counter-diagonals can portray the rush of movement across a picture surface. This can be seen in his depiction of a fire in the hilly landscape of Kyiv, in which no line is parallel to the picture frame (Fig. 9). Instead, Bohomazov believed that energy needs to be pictorialized as originating from within the work of art, and that every stroke should capture its directional forces. Unlike Italian Futurism, where lines of force penetrate beyond the edges of paintings, for Bohomazov, they end in concentrated peaks of painterly mass within the picture space. Rhythmic contours perpetuate the illusion of the continuity of movement and serve as a counterpoint to the linear diagonality generated from within the interior of the work. This singular principle of visual representation guided Bohomazov's art prior to his becoming a teacher at the Kyiv Art Institute. Finally, a short period of teaching in the Caucasus resulted in a sense of spectral colour that began to occupy him toward the end of his career in the latter part of the 1920s.

'Spectralism' is a term also associated with the art of Viktor Palmov (Fig. 10), who came to Kyiv in 1925 at the invitation of the Kyiv Art Institute, after having spent more than a decade in association with Futurist poets, and after a Futurist tour of Japan, Siberia, and the Far East with his fellow countryman Davyd Burliuk.

9
Oleksandr Bohomazov
Fire, **1916**
Lead pencil on paper
27 × 31.7 cm
National Art Museum
of Ukraine, Kyiv

Palmov's earlier works responded to a synthetic current labelled Cubo-Futurism, which mostly focused on geometric form but infused with dynamic movement. When he was appointed professor of painting at the Institute, Palmov came with first-hand experience and knowledge of Futurism, but turned his attention to the study of colour. Like Bohomazov, Palmov theorized about 'colour-writing', which he described in detail in the Panfuturist journal, *Nova Heneratsiia*.

Bohomazov's peer and fellow Kyivan, the future world-class Modernist sculptor Oleksandr Arkhypenko (also known as Alexander Archipenko, 1887–1964), had his first one-man show in his native Ukraine in 1906. By 1910, he was exhibiting in Paris, where he became an active member of La Section d'Or, and by 1920 he had an individual show at the Venice Biennale. Merging relief and painting, and using various materials, including stucco and polychrome wood, he created a hybrid style of 'sculpto-painting' that explored Cubism's plasticity. While abroad, Arkhypenko set up his first school in Berlin and continued to teach even after immigrating to the United States in 1923, where he became a central figure of the American avant-garde.

The daring, experimental steps taken by these artists contrast sharply with Kharkiv Futurism, whose practitioners, in both lifestyle and worldview, represented a far more bohemian aspect of Ukrainian Modernism. At the heart of the eastern avant-garde was Maria Syniakova (1890–1984), whose sensuous paintings epitomize the lifestyle of an artistic colony that, from the onset of the First World War, gathered during the summers at her family hamlet at Krasna Poliana outside the city. The

Oleksandr Arkhypenko
The Bather, 1915
Oil paint, graphite, paper,
and metal on panel
50.8 × 29.2 cm
Philadelphia Museum of Art,
United States

12
Maria Syniakova
War, 1916
Graphite pencil, India ink,
and gouache on paper
30.3 × 20.5 cm
Private collection, Kyiv

verdant, idyllic setting of the rural environs gave licence to uninhibited artistic and
poetic activity that did not set out so much to challenge convention as it did to tap
into a rich reservoir of creative energy. Stimulated largely by the fertile surroundings
of the Ukrainian countryside and an innate curiosity about distant and past
cultures, Syniakova's Modernist vision was a blend of the euphoric and decorative
in compositions that recall the intimate tableaux of Persian miniatures. The sensual
nature of her imagery is as liberating as the utopian promises of modernity were
fleeting. Like magic carpets coursing through time, her genteel works on paper
capture both the transcendent and the catastrophic. As she exposes the suddenness
of modern war that wilfully disturbed an organic, sensorial relationship with the
peaceful environment surrounding Kharkiv (Fig. 12), Syniakova's works have
a profound resonance today in the context of the 2022 assault on Ukraine.

Boichukism

The 'Boichukists' followed the ideas of the artist Mykhailo Lvovych Boichuk (1882–1937), who propagated a Byzantine aesthetic consonant with Ukraine's eastern Christian inheritance. In the cradle of Modernist movements in Paris in the 1910s, Boichuk launched his unique approach to modern painting, which contemporary critics such as Guillaume Apollinaire identified as the 'School of Byzantine Revival'. Together with émigré followers, the 'school' exhibited at the Salon d'Automne (1909) and the Salon des Indépendants (1910). Initially schooled in Vienna, Kraków, Munich, and then Paris, Boichuk was well-travelled and had become well-versed in the art of Italian proto-Renaissance artists, most notably Giotto. Wartime developments temporarily curtailed his artistic aspirations and, upon his return to Ukraine, Boichuk primarily engaged in the restoration of icons. After the collapse of the Russian Empire and the declaration of Ukraine's independence, he moved to Kyiv to become one of the original faculty of the newly formed Ukrainian Academy of Art in 1917. Boichuk headed the studio of monumental painting, which explored ancient techniques of tempera and fresco painting, while applying these techniques to a modern and contemporary context. Drawing on the loyalty and talent of his students, Boichuk abandoned panel painting in exchange for mural art and organized a brigade of his pupils, among whom was the artist Vasyl Sedliar, and a representative contingent of female artists – which, alongside his wife Sofia Nalepynska-Boichuk, included Maria Kotliarevska, Antonina Ivanova, and the most renowned, Oksana Pavlenko, if only to name a few. Together they carried out commissions of government-sponsored monumental and agit-art projects in the spirit of the tendentious propaganda themes of the new Bolshevik regime. The collective work of the Boichukists could be seen in community centres throughout Soviet-occupied Ukraine, including in Odesa and in the Bolshevik-established capital of Soviet Ukraine – Kharkiv.

In 1921, the Boichukists decorated Kharkiv in preparation for the upcoming Fifth All-Ukrainian Congress of Soviets. This event marked an important turning point in the art history of modern Ukraine, for it brought together two major currents of Modernist activity representing disparate orientations: Boichukism and Constructivism. The collaboration of Boichuk and Vasyl Yermylov in decorating Kharkiv's Liebknecht Street as a festive greeting for the visiting members of the Congress ultimately led to the formation of the Association of Revolutionary Art

13
Mykhailo Boichuk
The Cry of Yaroslavna,
sketch for mural, early 1910s
Cardboard, tempera, gold leaf
40 × 34 cm
Borys Voznytskyi Lviv
National Art Gallery

'Boichuk [...] propagated a Byzantine aesthetic consonant with Ukraine's eastern Christian inheritance.'

ГШАН AΠΟΛΛΑΡ

'Together [the Boichukists] carried out commissions of government-sponsored monumental and agit-art projects in the spirit of the tendentious propaganda themes of the new Bolshevik regime.'

15
Ivan Padalka
Photographer in the Village, 1927
Tempera on paper
33.5 × 45 cm
National Art Museum
of Ukraine, Kyiv

of Ukraine, known as ARMU. This association synthesized the diverse approaches to contemporary Ukrainian art into a unified Modernist position during the active period of Sovietization of the country in the 1920s.

Boichuk's protégé Ivan Padalka (1894–1937) revived the ceramics industry with a Modernist orientation, establishing production workshops and studios in Myrhorod, as well as in Mezhyhiria, near Kyiv. Despite attempts on the part of the Boichukists to guide Ukraine's agrarian population toward the newly imposed Soviet ideology, be it through the introduction of literacy into villages (as shown by Sedliar, Fig. 14) or through the use of photography to document progress (as demonstrated by Padalka's painting, Fig. 15), Boichuk and his followers were ultimately charged with treachery for promoting national identity through a style and form founded on past models of religious art. Labelled derisively as 'bourgeois nationalists', Padalka, along with other Boichukists, was executed as part of the Stalinist purges. Most of the murals and artwork of the Boichukists have been destroyed. Only a handful of examples, largely tempera on paper, have been preserved. Boichukism, as a Ukrainian avant-garde movement, is known primarily through photographic documents.

Richly decorated earthenware bowls and shallow bowls of different depths constitute the oldest form of Ukrainian ceramics. These products had a wide range of functions and were usually placed on a special shelf to decorate traditional interiors. During important meals they were put out on the table, and on big holidays like Christmas and Easter, they were taken to church.

Simple, unpretentiously decorated bowls of various sizes were used
in everyday life for cooking, washing, and eating food. Urban influences
gradually made their mark on folk ceramics, and in addition to painted
bowls, potters began to make flat decorative plates. See page 242.

ART DURING
THE SOVIET ERA

1930s to 1980s

Oleksandr Soloviev

U krainian art of the Soviet era – which was not just part of the Soviet agenda, but its flagship – came to an end with the collapse of the USSR. Its history is controversial and complex, and is still in the process of being written. There are still many blind spots and gaps to fill in, and it is difficult to fully understand all its nuances and to describe it objectively. For most of the period, Ukrainian art existed in isolation, and as a result was distorted – anomalous in its development and detached from what was taking place outside the borders of the USSR, a country that believed it was building a socialist society. Strict ideological control went hand-in-hand with state support for producing 'correct' art, which in turn provided many privileges and bonuses for those who did so. When the time came to dismantle this system (a process that continues to this day), many names were retrieved from oblivion, and as a response to injustice, many former 'heroes' were taken down from their pedestals.

The 1920s were a time of vigorous artistic and cultural exploration in Ukraine. A variety of artistic directions, schools, and associations brought intense competition and led to substantial creative output. Among these associations were those that inherited realist traditions of the Wanderers, like the Association of Artists of Red Ukraine (AKhChU). But the organizations that prevailed were those oriented toward the search for new forms, such as the Association of Revolutionary Art of Ukraine (ARMU), the Union of Contemporary Artists of Ukraine (OSMU), or October (Zhovten). Most of the artists in these groups sincerely wanted to participate in the grandiose transformations of society professed by the Soviet leadership and to use their art to build a new way of life and a new type of citizen. They saw the potential for this in a different kind of artistic tradition from the critical realism of the nineteenth century. Artists turned instead to the avant-garde, which had established itself in the art world a decade earlier – especially since it, too, aimed for a radical reorganization of the world. The avant-garde movement significantly influenced the development of these Ukrainian art collectives. For example, artists such as Kostiantyn Yeleva and Vasyl Sedliar continued to use the radical language of painting right up to the first half of the 1930s. This was also seen in the works featured in a large exhibition called 'Spetsfond' ('secret storage') that was held at the National Art Museum of Ukraine in 2015. A secret storage facility was created at the museum between 1937 to 1939, and all the works in it had been earmarked for destruction during those years, but they have nevertheless survived.

Some groups maintained that monumental art was superior to art painted on an easel. Mykhailo Boichuk and his students, the Boichukists, painted original murals, relying on historical styles such as the Italian Quattrocento, French Cubism, Byzantine art, and Ukrainian folk art. The last glimpses of avant-garde art could be seen in Kharkiv, the Ukrainian capital at the time, where Vasyl Yermylov was actively developing his own vision of Constructivism. It was here, too, that the Constructivist scenography of Oleksandr Khvostenko-Khvostov, Vadym Meller, and Anatol Petrytskyi had emerged.

In the 1930s, after the Central Committee of the Communist Party of the Soviet Union's decision to 'restructure' literary and artistic organizations, various associations were abolished and attention turned to artists who wholly supported the ideological and political platform of the Communist Party. Artistic diversity was replaced by a unified movement of socialist realism – art that ostensibly reflected Soviet life and its revolutionary development in a truthful way. In practice, however, it was not revolutionary but archaic traditions, propagated by artists of AKhChU, that took centre stage. Karpo Trokhymenko's *Builders of the Dnipro Hydroelectric Station* (1937), with its attractive yet superficial realism, can in many ways be considered the embodiment of this style. The artists of this period were eventually forced to abandon any semblance of realistic documentation. Live scenes, from which artists would have painted on location, were replaced by staged mise-en-scènes composed of models in a studio, put together according to a classical framework. And then, the Great Purge began, in both life and art.

At the end of the 1930s, the masters of the Monumental school, headed by Boichuk, were executed. Thus, the unique movement of Ukrainian Monumentalists – with their elevated concern for the form of art and their developed methods of training future artists – ceased to exist. Their names were erased from the history of Ukrainian art for almost thirty years. In official propaganda, they became symbols representing the notorious ideologies of 'formalism' and 'militant bourgeois nationalism'. The 1930s left many interesting trends in ruins and ended the careers of numerous artists of outstanding talent, thrown to the sidelines of the contemporary art world. But many artists adapted to the circumstances of the prevailing situation. This is how the extremely gifted graphic artist Vasyl Kasiian, at one time close to the Boichukists due to his participation in ARMU, quickly and irrevocably became a socialist realist, and for many years occupied leading positions in Ukrainian Soviet graphic arts – largely losing the originality of his style in the process. During the Second World War, as during the Russian Civil War (c. 1918–22), the most in-demand genres and types of art became those that were malleable, capable of responding with lightning speed to current events and rousing the masses to resistance and victory: posters, graphic sketches, propaganda and mass art, as well as patriotic paintings created within the established canonical framework.

The main features of socialist realism revealed themselves in the period following the Second World War, when a new generation of artists came on the scene, many of them graduates of the National Academy of Visual Arts and Architecture in Kyiv. The range of imaginative themes and aesthetics included the everyday and the didactic

(as seen in paintings by Serhii Hryhoriev), ceremonial pomposity (exemplified in the works of Mykhailo Khmelko), and poster-like qualities (seen in paintings by Viktor Puzyrkov and Tetiana Yablonska – specifically her work *Bread*, 1949). Heorhii Melikhov's painting *Young Taras Shevchenko Visiting the Artist Karl Briullov* (1947) stands out for its highly picturesque qualities. Ukrainian painters were actively involved in the All-Union art exhibitions of the late 1940s and early 1950s, and many were awarded state prizes (then called Stalin prizes), but this success had a downside. Those artists who distinguished themselves with their first works seemed to stall, trying to repeat their achievements, and their students tried to follow the same well-trodden path. By the 1950s, a false stereotype had developed of Ukrainian artists as masters of exceptionally large canvases, dominated by narratives on significant Soviet themes. Yablonska alone managed perhaps to evolve beyond these strict conventions, but it was only in the late 1950s, and especially in the 1960s, that she became fascinated by Ukrainian folklore and critics started talking about the 'new Yablonska'.

Following the death of Stalin, the canonical period of socialist realism ended, and the Khrushchev Thaw began (a period when repression and censorship was relaxed). With it came a relative widening of the scope of formal approaches and the birth of new phenomena, such as the flourishing of the so-called 'Sixtiers'. While officially, their art was defined by its rough style, unofficially it was clearly Nonconformist.

Brezhnev, the USSR's next leader, ushered in what is often called the Era of Stagnation, during which artists, in order to be exhibited and for their works to be purchased by the state, had to create countless visual 'documents' about the quasi-victories of socialism and the joyful working lives of Soviet citizens. The whole Soviet Union – and Ukraine was no exception – was covered with enormous monuments. At major exhibitions, Ukrainian artists seemed the most careful to follow the canons of socialist realism, with the exception of a few painters from the Lviv and Uzhhorod art schools, where European painting traditions had not yet been completely eradicated.

In 1976, a party resolution on working with creative youth was adopted, and at high-profile exhibitions of young artists, participants enjoyed a little more freedom than they could at adult exhibitions, which were very difficult to get in to, held in pharaonic halls, often tied to Soviet milestone celebrations, and featured huge commissioned paintings by those artists favoured by the authorities. At the youth exhibitions, on the other hand, deviations from accepted normative aesthetics were allowed, up to a certain point. A new term even appeared: 'permitted art'. It was at these exhibitions that Serhii Geta's large-format paintings were shown, along with Serhii Bazylev's photorealist paintings (reflecting a leading trend in Western art at the time, which the Soviet Union itself was close to legalizing). These exhibitions were also the first outing for the colourful paintings of Tiberii Silvashi, which he defined as chronorealism; it was on this stage too that, during Gorbachev's Perestroika period of political reforms, the New Wave movement proudly announced itself, introducing a whole generation of Ukrainian artists to global postmodernism. This was the final act in the history of Ukrainian art during the Soviet era. In December 1991, an agreement was signed in Belovezhskaia Pushcha (present-day Belarus) that marked the dissolution of the Soviet Union, and from then on, Ukraine continued its artistic development as an independent state.

Halls of Farewell at the Kyiv Crematorium
Avraam Miletskyi
(architect)
1968–81
Kyiv

Genre Painting

From the beginning of the 1930s, Ukrainian art suffered a noticeable decrease in the creative exploration associated with the avant-garde movement. As a unified Soviet statehood strengthened, demand grew for state-standardized art that served its emerging totalitarian ideology. The turning point was the invention, declaration, and dissemination of a single movement for all Soviet art – socialist realism. Of the entire spectrum of artistic traditions, only one style was sanctioned: the realist art typical of the Peredvizhniki (the Wanderers) in the second half of the nineteenth century. What followed was a clear hierarchy of genres and themes. The lowest genres were condemned in every possible way by firmly established Communist Party critics; the party was especially vociferous against landscape painting of the 1930s. On the other hand, works aimed at the visual exaltation of the emerging cult of personality around Stalin, as well as genres and themes that glorified both the heroic national past (above all, the revolutionary past), and the heroic Soviet present (especially feats of labour) were held in the highest regard. Not all artists could make it into this elite caste. Of course, not all artists wanted to be a part of it, since such a moral compromise was fraught with artistic trade-offs. It was at precisely this time that a saving grace came to the aid of artists reluctant to submit to the dictates of this heroic art: a secondary genre in the emerging hierarchy – the art of everyday life, a kind of Soviet Biedermeier based on the Wanderers' tradition. This genre was not only welcomed, but came to stand front and centre in the art scene. It was in this genre that many artists saw an alternative to the Stalinist Empire style and an early outlet for quiet disagreement with the official narrative. The genre was closely tied to folk life and the mundane, and its unpretentious format did not interfere with its main objective: narration, storytelling, and full-scale verisimilitude. By the 1950s, however, this genre, too, began to be glorified, and then came its sharp decline and degeneration into almost anecdotal marginality.

This political and artistic context is needed in order to understand the appearance and meaning of the genre painting *Miner's Love* (1935), painted by Fedir Krychevskyi after his trip to the Donbas. He had planned to paint a whole series of works called *Youth of Donbas*, but *Miner's Love* remained its first and only work. Krychevskyi was an important figure in Ukrainian art. He began painting even before the Soviet period, and in the 1920s his art experienced its heyday – his 1927 triptych *Life*, in which Art Nouveau influences are noticeable, was shown in the same year at the Venice Biennale. Krychevskyi's easel works are distinguished by the grandeur of their composition, broad brushstrokes, and depictions of national character. While remaining true to realist painting, he was simultaneously able to introduce decorative elements thanks to his passion for European schools of art, trends, and styles such as Art Nouveau (he was especially fond of the Austrian Gustav Klimt and the Swiss Ferdinand Hodler), Symbolism, Impressionism, and Post-Impressionism. In the same

1
Fedir Krychevskyi
Miner's Love, 1935
183 × 175 cm
National Art Museum
of Ukraine, Kyiv

year as *Miner's Love*, Krychevskyi painted *Conquerors of Wrangel*. This large painting had a historical, revolutionary theme: he used principles of classical Deisis paintings (Byzantine icon representations of Christ) but with new subjects – the heroes of the Russian Civil War, which also engulfed Ukraine after the Russian Revolution of 1917. Nevertheless, it was the artist's preference for genre painting that became predominant in his work in the 1930s, such as *Merry Milkmaids*, 1937. Although both this and *Miner's Love* are depictions of labour, they lack the excessive degree of praise and falsity characteristic of works that espoused the Soviet official narrative. What comes to the fore in these paintings are their sculptural and colouristic qualities, typical traits of the genre (a domestic scene), and the overall humanistic sense. His large-scale images are more reminiscent of staged productions – this is very typical of Krychevskyi in every phase of his career. In *Miner's Love*, unpretentious colouring supports the lyrical narrative of the work. The motif of a tryst was fairly widespread even before Krychevskyi's time, and has an established iconography among both domestic and international artists: the Ukrainian member of the Wanderers Mykola

Pymonenko; the Italian neo-academicist Eugene de Blaas with his painting *The Spider and the Fly* (1889); the French Auguste Renoir; and of course, Jules Bastien-Lepage, also French, whose painting *Love in the Village* (1882) evokes the closest associations with Krychevskyi's mise-en-scène.

Tetiana Yablonska was a student of Krychevskyi and, like him, she was also a genre painter. Her artistic experiments were interrupted by the Second World War, and she was only able to resume her work after returning to Kyiv in 1944. A special place in her oeuvre is occupied by the genre painting *Before the Start* (1947), which clearly shows the young artist's passion for Impressionism. Yablonska was mercilessly criticized for this in the Stalinist newspaper *Culture and Life*: Formalism, and Impressionism in particular, were considered manifestations of bourgeois culture and had no place in socialist art. The influence of Impressionism was felt not only in terms of the work's spontaneity, but also in Yablonska's approach to depicting such a sprawling, multi-dimensional scene – specifically, the almost inadvertent cropping and spontaneous fragmentation of her composition. This work is remarkable in that, like her epic painting *Bread* created two years later, it reflects the optimism of the post-war period. Ease, joy, and warmth define the mood of this work; its plein-air authenticity and narrative development are secondary to the most important thing – the artist's ability to encapsulate her own feelings and depict them meaningfully. This type of inspirational, impulsive painting style is closely integrated with the structural consistency of the whole. In the composition, the principle of dynamic diagonal lines is used, which gives the image movement. Such an approach – the juxtaposition of

2
Tetiana Yablonska
***Before the Start**, 1947*
Oil on canvas
126 × 210 cm
National Art Museum
of Ukraine, Kyiv

3
Serhii Hryhoriev
Admission to the Komsomol, **1949**
Oil on canvas
Original version

two visual planes, the close-up foreground, and the distant background with its high horizon line – achieves depth within the painting. This contrast is further reinforced by each plane's artistic qualities: the subtle contrast of warm and cold shades, and the blending of colour families and vivid highlights.

Another student of Krychevskyi was Serhii Hryhoriev, a recognized master of genre painting. Among his usual motifs are meetings, collective discussions, and Soviet rituals; these can be seen in the paintings *Admission to the Komsomol* (1949), *Discussion of the Deuce* (1950) and *Parents' Meeting* (1960). Like Yablonska, Hryhoriev worked from natural impressions when painting *Admission to the Komsomol*. This work was exemplary of its time, as it combined the vitality of the genre with the prescriptions of socialist realism. It depicts the typical ritual of admission to the ranks of Komsomol members, a political organization for educating young people about Communist ideals. Hryhoriev overshadows the moment's sense of formality and protocol through a greater emphasis on emotion and the psychological. The characters are drawn together in a common action, facilitated by the recurring use of red, the symbolic colour of the Soviet banner (which the artist managed to use for purely formal purposes). However, the presence of Stalin, here in the form of a bust, was at the time a prerequisite for such a scene. It is no coincidence that the painting was originally called *Admission to the Komsomol. Stalinist Tribe*. After the painting was awarded the Stalin Prize of the 2nd degree, it was acquired by the National Museum. But in the later 1950s, when Stalin's cult of personality had been debunked, the artist painted over his bust. Currently, the painting lies in the storerooms of the National Museum, and its original version can only be seen in reproductions.

The Poetics of Colour and Light

Of all the different Ukrainian art forms that existed in the Soviet era, painting is easily the most prominent. It was through this form that the main Soviet dogmas were most openly communicated, especially through narrative and thematic paintings. Experimentation with avant-garde ideas were also most clearly visible in paintings, beginning in the first Soviet decade – the 1920s – and after a long break, in the 1960s among Nonconformist artists. Between these two timeframes ran another throughline of painters who explored the nature of this art form (though they were not as radical as, say, the Abstractionists of the late 1950s and 70s) and were concerned with finding techniques with which to express movement using elements such as colour and light.

Pavlo Holubiatnykov was a consistent champion of the principles of his teacher and friend Kuzma Petrov-Vodkin. This affinity was manifested in his use of a spherical perspective, complex angles and the combination of different viewpoints, icon-like faces, concentrated colour, and a reliance on the legacy of the Renaissance. Importantly, for both artists, painting was a way of thinking – a philosophy, and not just an instrumental space for formal exploration. However, Holubiatnykov did eventually come to develop a technically complex optical system that he called 'light painting'. From there, his work aspired to the spiritual, which, according to him, was the only basis of creation. These qualities can be seen in his paintings from his Kyiv period, from 1925 to 1930. At this time, he taught at the Kyiv Art Institute, together with Kazimir Malevich and Volodymyr Tatlin, and was a member of the Association of Revolutionary Art of Ukraine and later, OSMU, a group that focused precisely on this quest for creating movement in their work. Holubiatnykov also participated in the 1928 Venice Biennale. The best works from his Kyiv period include *Kyiv Girl* (1925–26), *Woman's Head* (1926), and *Children in the Garden* (1928), in which the iconographic arrangement of the Trinity is easily observable.

During this same period, new themes appeared in his work, reflecting the intrusion of patriarchal structures into the realities of Soviet industrialization, specifically in the paintings *Aeroplane over the Village* (1927) and *Tractors* (1928). These paintings are characterized by an increase in distortion: the manipulation of visual planes is accentuated, the angularity of objects is dramatized, and the use of colour is more and more stylized, its symbolic significance coming to the fore. All of these elements created paintings full of drama and tension, as everyday scenes became timeless. The image of a tractor became very common in Ukrainian paintings. Dubbed the 'steel horse', the tractor was emblematic of the changing times and new way of life. In *Tractors*, modernity is in tension with archaic styles, as seen in the icon-like interpretations of the people. The procession of tractors has started far in the distance, and moving toward the viewer, it forms an axis in the composition, intersecting with different spaces and perspectives. The blue colour of both the trees and the tractors gives the picture a sense of unreality and fantasy.

4
Pavlo Holubiatnykov
Tractors, 1928
Oil on canvas
140 × 125 cm
National Art Museum
of Ukraine, Kyiv

5
Mykola Hlushchenko
Rest, 1973
Oil on canvas
100 × 80 cm
Private collection

Mykola Hlushchenko was another excellent colourist. It was colour that formed the beginning of all his paintings – it filled his canvases with movement and ornamentality. And yet, it is impossible to deny his work's naturalness, despite his improvisational method of painting: its effortless organization, the balance of tonal relationships, and the rich textural play. Hlushchenko developed his professional credo based on European painting traditions. In the first half of the 1920s, he studied art in Berlin, and in 1925 he moved to Paris, where he worked for a long time, having been influenced by the French Impressionists. The painting style of such artists as Manet, Monet, Renoir, and Bonnard, with its colour and luminosity, is evident in many of Hlushchenko's works. Despite this, he cannot be called a mere imitator: his work has its own inner poetics, and he has his own style of applying bold, multidirectional and, as it were, messy brushstrokes. Landscape was the artist's favourite genre, but he also often depicted female nudes, and not only in painting (see, for example, his acclaimed album of erotic lithographs of 1928). In his series of nude paintings, what stands out are his masterful brushstrokes and colouristic perfection. In the 1970s, during the last years of his life, he painted *Rest* (Fig. 5, p. 199), *Nude on the Sofa*, and *Artist and Model. Self-Portrait with a Nude*. The nude genre in these and other works of the series is mixed with elements from other genres – the still life, the self-portrait, the interior scene – which expanded and enriched their imagery.

In the 1970s, the Odesan artist Yurii Yehorov painted several paintings under the same title, *Leaving Soon*. The sea motifs in the artist's work are not accidental, but are features of his mythological world. In his paintings, the sea is always alive, frothy, and textured, with a curved, sparkling horizon line permeated with sunlight. For Yehorov, light is the very basis of the visible world, its prototype, which exists on a metaphysical level. As a rule, his paintings are backlit, providing a clear separation between light and shadow, while also allowing the tonal range to go from darkest to lightest with many gradations of colour. The motif of departure – the invitation to travel into the unknown – is undeniably romantic. The white square of a maritime flag with a blue border, fluttering in the hands of a girl, indicates that the ship will soon raise its anchor and set sail. All of the painting's features – the girl that appears in it and the colour of her surroundings (the sea and sky) – have well-defined symbolic interpretations. In particular, the sea is symbolic of perpetual motion, constant changeability, and mystery, while the sky is the embodiment of the cosmos and the divine.

The search for movement in painting can also be seen in the painting *Jars* (1985), created by another 'magician of light and colour', Anatolii Lymariev. The painting glows from the inside out: its hot yellow-orange colour scheme, with splashes of contrasting greens and reinforcing reds, blurry silhouettes, and the dark spot of a sitting figure in the foreground all contribute to the appearance of a rich atmosphere in this vivid image-experience. These details turn a simple scene into a sublime and mysterious narrative.

7
Anatolii Lymariev
***Jars*, 1985**
Oil on canvas
97 × 107 cm
Courtesy of the artist's family

Nonconformist Artists

With the onset of the Khrushchev Thaw in the second half of the 1950s, both political and cultural oppression in the Soviet Union was slightly loosened. Soviet art, in all its constituent countries, had been in complete isolation for almost three decades. Moreover, many of its representatives had not only been subjected to ideological 're-education' but also in some cases executed. It was not possible to eliminate all objectionable artists, however, so some still worked – even if it was just to put their creations in a drawer – at the risk of their careers and lives. Others produced work in line with global art trends, albeit lagging behind and of a different ilk, since they could only look inward for inspiration. All this was, of course, surreptitious, as well as sporadic; it developed individually rather than collectively. Nevertheless, the seed of an alternative vision to the prevailing ideology of socialist realism could not help but take root. In 1957, many foreign delegations arrived at the World Festival of Youth and Students in Moscow, where there was a large exhibition programme. Just two years later, a Picasso exhibition was organized there. This may not have been true freedom, but it was still a breath of fresh air, and had an effect on the overall trajectory of artistic development. It was then that several new artistic movements began throughout the Soviet Union, including in Ukraine. One of these movements was Nonconformism, which gained strength at the turn of the 1960s. In the common cultural understanding, this style was associated with dissidence.

Among the Nonconformist artists in Ukraine at the time, one of the most influential was Anatolii Sumar, a professional architect who devoted himself to experiments in painting. He produced about fifty works, in which real and abstract motifs were intertwined. All of his experimental works were made during a short six-year period. After accusations of formalism, he stopped painting. What is striking about Sumar's work (as well as in that of several other Nonconformist artists) is his mastery of other art forms, and his lack of fear about experimenting with different media. Another prominent representative of this movement, Hryhorii Havrylenko, was an excellent book illustrator, notably of works by Dante. His second passion, hidden in those years from the general public, was abstract painting – sometimes expressive, and at other times more minimalist, with geometric splashes of colour. Havrylenko began experimenting with abstract forms in the late 1960s, calling them 'non-objective' works. In his later cycles, to which *Composition* (1981) belongs, he strove to create a harmony of simple forms; an atmosphere of complete unity. This is not a static state; the elements seem to float to the top of the image surface, as if they have their own hidden dynamics. Havrylenko paid particular attention to the relationship between light and colour in this work. The bright, open colours hold a sort of luminous power, and the transparency achieved in the painting endows these elements with light and airiness.

Valerii Lamakh, another artist of the same period, was officially assigned to monumental art and poster production by the state, but in the late 1950s he also

8
Hryhorii Havrylenko
Composition, 1982
Watercolour on paper
38.5 × 28.1 cm
Collection of Edward Dymshyts

began to create abstract paintings in the expressionist style. By the end of the 1960s, he began his master work, *Books of Schemes*, in which he discussed aesthetics from the point of view of a visual artist, but mainly as a thinker and poet (Fig. 9, p. 204). Lamakh managed to create five books, but the work remained unfinished upon his death in 1978. Lamakh came to philosophy through intuition and contemplation. He was inspired by the idea that all existence was dynamically interconnected; he came up with a complete concept of the world, then translated it to visual form. Today, it is obvious that he was a conceptual artist: it is no coincidence that in 2017 a fragment of his *Books* was included in the contemporary art exhibition 'documenta 14' in Germany.

The artists mentioned above worked in Kyiv, but that was not the only place the Nonconformist movement thrived. Many artists in Lviv deserve attention too,

9
Valerii Lamakh
From the fourth *Book of Schemes*
1969–79
(Album #2, third folder)
Gouache on paper
25 × 19 cm
Private collection

especially since the city is a unique case – it was a late addition to the USSR in 1939. Several artists in Lviv had received western European educations, such as Margit Selska and her husband, Roman Selsky. A group of students formed around them who were open to Modernist traditions and even contemporary trends. Among them was Karlo Zvirynskyi, who stood out for his abstract paintings as well as his relief paintings, in which he used the unconventional medium of metal. Since the second half of the 1950s, Zvirynskyi had been immersed in the search for so-called 'pure form', devoid of any recognizable associations. This led him to abstraction, to the expansion of technical and figurative methods, and to overcoming the flatness of the pictorial image. In his cycles *Verticals* and *Reliefs* (including *Tin*; Fig. 10), Zvirynskyi achieved the unique concept of 'tactile abstraction', through the heavy use of texture in a variety of materials – wood, tin, plaster, lace, paper, and glue.

Petro Markovych, another painter from Lviv, pondered the advances of twentieth-century art around the world and created his own (somewhat naive) take on them. Elements of Dadaism and Surrealism appeared in his works of the 1960s. In his assemblages, each object was endowed with a memory and laden with a specific poetic meaning. *Madonna* is part of his series of 'button images' created between 1966 and 1968 (Fig. 11, p. 206). In similar assemblages, such as *Black Flowers* (1967), buttons were used as a three-dimensional component to recreate his impressions of a crematorium.

Outstanding Nonconformist artists could also be found in Uzhhorod, including Pavlo Bedzir, Ferents Seman, and Yelyzaveta Kremnytska. A native of Vinnytsia oblast, Feodosii Humeniuk worked intermittently in Dnipro and St Petersburg from the 1960s to the 1980s. He continued the Byzantine inclination in painting revived by the school of Mykhailo Boichuk. Focusing on colour, composition, and canvas texture, he developed a style that combined archaic Ukrainian symbols and modern painting techniques, for which he was persecuted by those in power.

The city of Odesa also needs particular consideration: it is the only city in Ukraine, and one of the few in the Soviet Union, where during the 1960s to the 1980s there existed not only independent (and good) artists, but a whole alternative art world, including art schools, groups, new generations of artists, and different specialisms. Odesa went through several waves of Nonconformism. This can be traced back to the 1950s, beginning with Teofil Fraierman, who lived in Paris for many years and was, in the eyes of many Odesa artists, a living exemplar of European painting culture, as well as an ethical role model as a politically unbiased artist. Another important figure was Oleh Sokolov, who created small 'chamber' works (works of very small size, shown mainly in artists' own apartments) and abstract compositions in which he explored the idea of synthesizing painting and music.

10
Karlo Zvirynskyi
Tin, **1959**
Plywood, tin, paint
46.5 × 72 cm
Private collection

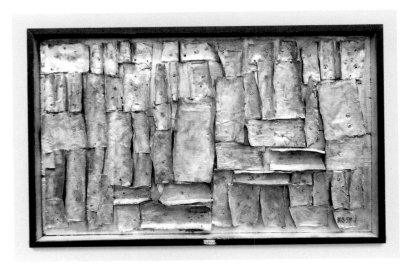

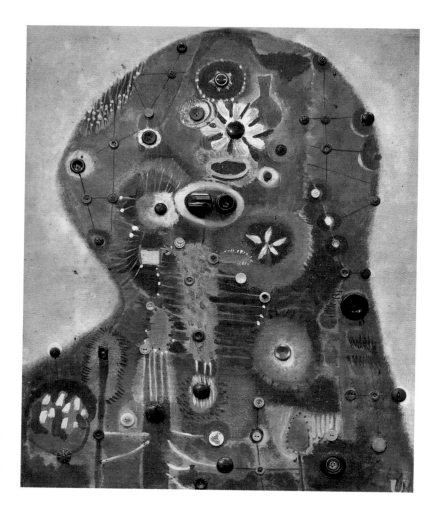

11
Petro Markovych
Madonna, **1967**
Oil on cardboard, collage
75 × 61 cm
Borys Voznytskyi Lviv National
Art Gallery

In the 1960s, art moved more toward painting: Volodymyr Naumets, Liudmyla Yastreb, Valentyn Khrushch, Volodymyr Strelnikov, Oleksandr Anufriev, Valerii Basanets, Viktor Mariniuk, and others were looking for a way to be expressive within the framework of easel paintings, and images no larger than a metre were most prevalent. This format called for an appropriate exhibition style: the 'apartment exhibition', in which all the artworks were arranged in 'gallery walls', with the entire surface of a wall covered in paintings. Strelnikov's *Fisherman's House* (1970) is a quintessential work from his last years in Odesa, in which he frequently depicted views of its landscape. When Strelnikov left Odesa for Munich, he moved away from figurative painting and began to engage in abstraction. The beginnings of this shift are just noticeable in this small, but very expressive work, in its minimal use of colour and form. The white house on the seashore becomes a poetic metaphor through the painter's brush, hinting at the mysterious life behind its niche windows.

It was in Odesa that, for the first time in the USSR, an interactive 'guerrilla' exhibition took place in a public urban space. Long before the dramatic events of the 1974 Bulldozer Exhibition in Moscow (an unauthorized exhibition on the streets of Moscow that was dispersed using water cannons and bulldozers), in the summer of 1964, Valentyn Khrushch and Stanislav Sychov hung their works on a fence in the Palais-Royal Garden in Odesa. The exhibition lasted for several hours before it was taken down by the police, who were assisted by Komsomol (the Young Communist League) do-gooders.

The second wave of Odesa Nonconformism was conceptual. It originated at the turn of the 1980s. The first to play a major role in its development were artists Leonid Voitsekhov, Serhii Anufriev, Yurii Leiderman, Ihor Chatskin, and the group Pertsy (Liudmyla Skrypkyna and Oleh Petrenko). One important feature of this wave was the noticeable influence of Odesa lore, local dialect, and vernacular. This type of art was a product of the artist's inclinations – spontaneous, light, and ephemeral – and the work that resulted was almost secondary. Odesa conceptualism was not charged with direct social or political criticism; rather, the dissidence of Odesans was implied internally. Their work avoided open mockery of the Soviet state, though sadly this did not protect them from the all-seeing eyes of the KGB.

42
Volodymyr Strelnikov
***Fisherman's House*, 1970**
Oil on canvas
75 × 90 cm
Collection of Anatoly Dymchuk

The Art of Photography

In the post-war period, photography became a very common pastime throughout the Soviet Union, and Ukraine was no exception. When it came to professional reporters, they generally photographed stories in an extremely optimistic light. Their photographs were meant to capture an embellished version of life and propagandize party ideology – saturated to its core with socialist dogmas. In these photographs the idea of the collective was of course dominant. Such a widespread hobby also gave rise to a large wave of amateur photographers who united in clubs and groups where they could improve their skills. There were also groups of professional photographers who inevitably began to be weighed down by the ideological mission of their beloved work. In the late 1950s, various subcultural movements began to appear, in which photography's role was to immortalize all kinds of events. In Kharkiv, a group was formed called the Blue Horse – an underground youth association that professed a bohemian creative life, sexual freedom, and nudism – but its members were soon arrested and received various prison sentences. It was no coincidence that Kharkiv became Soviet Ukraine's epicentre of interest in a completely different type of photography, not so much connected to its possibilities as a tool of documentation, but to its aesthetic qualities, and as a means of critically rethinking reality. Kharkiv was an industrially and intellectually developed city, with many factories, engineers, and students. In the early Soviet years, it was the capital of Ukraine, home to many avant-garde artists, especially Constructivist artists. In the mid-1960s, at the end of the Khrushchev Thaw – with its burst of romanticism followed by the hard times of the Brezhnev Stagnation – Borys Mykhailov, an engineer at a Kharkiv factory, began to make a film about the times in which he lived. Working on the film gave him the impetus to work in photography. His series, including *Red Series* (1968–75), *Unfinished Thesis* (1984–85), and *Luriki* (1971–85), exposed an existential nerve of the time and its heroes, honestly capturing their reality. Mykhailov's heroes and his reality were vastly different from the artificial, sugar-coated photographic depictions that were spread by the state and that had dominated for many years. In his writings, Mykhailov speaks about this in simple, but accurate terms: 'We lived in an in-between time, when heroism and pathos were lies. What mainly constituted this time, its historical feeling, was de-heroification, and an ironic and sceptical attitude toward life and ideology. At the same time, in this way of reflecting reality, there was an artistic levelling of the historical image.'

'Photographs were meant to capture an embellished version of life and propagandize party ideology – saturated to its core with socialist dogmas.'

In 1972, the group Vremia (Time) was formed in Kharkiv. Its members were Borys Mykhailov, Yurii Rupin, Yevhenii Pavlov, Oleh Malovanyi, Anatolii Makiienko, Oleksandr Suprun, Hennadii Tubaliev, and Oleksandr Sytnychenko. Each of these photographers maintained their own artistic independence, but the group as a whole also had a common idea, formulated as 'impact theory'. The goal was to stun, to stop the viewer, to 'turn on' their critical eyes, and to activate the defence mechanisms of pain and shock – like what follows a punch. Following this theory in practice radically changed the perception of photography, and legitimized this art form within a system that was traditionally recognized as highbrow. The group's activity took place underground, in a regime of constant restrictions and censorship bans. In reality, it was a semi-legal existence; suffice it to say that Vremia's only exhibition in Kharkiv did not take place until 1983 in the House of Scientists cultural centre, and was immediately shut down.

Often the photographer acted as a conscious provocateur, launching spontaneous performances and encouraging the subject to improvise. One example is Yevhenii Pavlov's *Violin* (1972), which was a revolutionary as well as lyrical series of staged photographs featuring a hippie; at the same time, it was a rare artistic experiment in depicting a naked male body. It should be noted that depicting nudity in Soviet photography was taboo, but for the members of Vremia, photographing nudes became the norm, shocking their contemporaries with their bravery. Another series in this vein is *Bathhouse* (1972) by Yurii Rupin. The very use of a photographic series, at a time when the format of single images still prevailed, was an innovation of the group, and expanded the artists' dialogue with their audience. After *Violin*, Yevhenii Pavlov shot another landmark series, *Love* (1976), and in 1988 he finally finished his *Archive Series*, begun in the mid-1960s: these were expressive black-and-white sketches, photographic documentations of Soviet life in Kharkiv (Fig. 13, p. 209). Although social issues were front and centre in the group's photographs, it was always difficult to truly discern whether they were documentary or staged shoots.

The artists could often achieve the illusion of spontaneous staging, even in candid shots. This blurring of boundaries had its own identifying features. Among other photographic techniques that were used by the group – and more widely, those that came out of the Kharkiv school of photography – were collage and montage. These techniques can be traced back to the Soviet avant-garde tradition of photomontage.

Another practice that gained popularity was the 'rehabilitation of kitsch', primarily seen in manually colourized photographs, with their bright, acid-like colour schemes stemming from anonymous folk photographs. Active experiments were also carried out with complex photographic techniques such as equidensity, the Sabattier effect, double exposure, and retouching. For example, Borys Mykhailov created the series *Yesterday's Sandwich* using the double exposure method. He began working on this series at a time when a photograph's aesthetic quality was not yet as important as it would become later. He was fascinated by playing with the possibilities of form: he would superimpose one image onto another and create unexpected spatial and structural effects, displacements, distortions, and diffusions, sometimes of an almost surrealistic nature. This gave rise to sequences of multifaceted artistic images with paradoxical metaphors and semantic overtones; in *Yesterday's Sandwich*, this can be seen in the overlapping spaces and the incongruous human ear on a city street.

14
Borys Mykhailov
From *Yesterday's Sandwich*,
late 1960s–early 1970s
Colour print
Courtesy of the artist

New Brutalism

The various periods of Ukrainian architecture that characterized the Soviet era differ in terms of their value, meaning, and aesthetic quality. After the Constructivist architecture of the 1920s, which left a significant mark on the general history of architecture, came the period of Stalinist architecture – a direct consequence of totalitarianism, and a time during which no notable monuments were erected. This, in turn, was followed by the popularity of architecture dominated by utilitarianism, austerity, and cookie-cutter housing developments. Finally, in the 1960s, as the country became more open, Ukrainian architecture began to focus on new trends spreading from western Europe. In Ukraine these were replicated almost at the same time as elsewhere in Europe. After many years of technological backwardness and the dominance of the 'Stalinist Empire', Soviet architects turned to the Roman orders, pomposity, and embellishment. One of the main trends was New Brutalism, developed by the Swiss-French architect Le Corbusier, whose technical principles for the use of reinforced concrete were put into practice by the German architect Friedrich Tamms. After the Second World War, New Brutalism was most consistently developed and utilized in the United Kingdom. Finally, this style began to be embraced in many other countries around the world.

Of particular interest was the architectural phenomenon in Kyiv from the 1960s to the 1980s, during which stylistic features of New Brutalism were clearly evident: the emphasized mass of enormous shapes, the boldness and complexity of architectural decisions while maintaining functionality, the absence of superfluous decor, a fixation on the sparse and severe qualities of the main building material – reinforced concrete – in its natural, brutal form, and an integrated approach that accentuated the urban nature of buildings. New Brutalist architecture could be seen in buildings of all kinds, including: the student buildings of the National Technical University (1973–84) and the Taras Shevchenko National University of Kyiv (1972–80); the Hlushkov Institute of Cybernetics (1973–77); Zhytnii Market (1980); the House of Furniture store (1971–84) with its concave roof, a detail characteristic of the era in Kyiv, and a concept likely borrowed from the popular Japanese architect Kenzo Tange; the Ukraina National Palace of Arts (1965–70); and the Vernadskyi National Library of Ukraine (1975–89; Fig. 15, p. 213). Key architects of the time included Mykhailo Budilovskyi, Natalia Chmutina, and Serhii Mirhorodskyi.

'Finally, in the 1960s, as the country became more open, Ukrainian architecture began to focus on new trends spreading from western Europe.'

'The interior of the library, with its imposing chandeliers, furniture, and accents, embodied almost every distinctive feature of the Soviet concept of beauty, which happened to include the same aesthetics as New Brutalism, with its fixation on being larger than life.'

Though the library blends organically into the urban environment, its twenty-seven-storey-high main block, where the library stacks are located, introduces an element of rhythmic dynamism in a structure that is otherwise static and monotonous. The decor of the library stacks was dictated by purely functional necessity – the thick latticework covering the main block reduces outside light, which is ideal for book storage. The interior of the library, with its imposing chandeliers, furniture, and stonework decorations, embodied almost every distinctive feature of the Soviet concept of beauty, which happened to include the same aesthetics as New Brutalism, with its fixation on being larger than life. It is no coincidence that these interiors were used as the filming location for many scenes in the famous American-British TV series *Chernobyl*.

One of the most iconic representatives of New Brutalism in Kyiv was Avraam Miletskyi, who designed the Salute hotel (1982–84), as well as the Halls of Farewell at the Kyiv Crematorium (1968–81), which are designed in the form of blossoming lotus petals – a Buddhist symbol of the eternal life of the soul (see p. 192). In this ritual construction, Miletskyi managed to bring to light the properties of raw concrete, especially its plasticity, which distinguished New Brutalism from earlier Modernism. Among the extraordinary Kyiv buildings in this style, the Ukrainian Institute of Scientific and Technical Expertise and Information (1965–71, architects: Florian Yuriev and Lev Novykov) must also be mentioned: the main expressive component of its design resembles a flying saucer. The image and the spherical shape were inspired by the ideas of cosmism – a philosophical movement very popular in the Soviet 1960s. It was conceived as a colour music theatre (a type of instrumental performance in which the colour signals generated by musical vibrations are translated into light) with unique acoustics. In this space, another vital idea was also visibly embodied – the synthesis of the arts, as music, theatre, architecture and monumental painting were interwoven.

15
Vernadskyi National Library
Vadym Hopkalo, Vadym Hrechyna, and Valerii Peskovskyi (architects)
1975–89
Kyiv

Summer Evening
20th century
Middle Dnipro, Poltava oblast
Oil on plywood
55 × 62.5 cm

Cossack Mamai
Undated
Kyiv

***People Go to Church
to Celebrate Easter***
20th century
Oil on canvas
59.3 × 80.2 cm

Young People by the River
20th century
Northeastern Ukraine
Oil on plywood
45.5 × 53 cm

*One of the most common subjects of Ukrainian folk paintings was the image of
the Cossack Mamai (a Ukrainian folk hero), depicted sitting in the middle of the
steppe holding a traditional Ukrainian instrument, a bandura. See page 242.*

CONTEMPORARY ART

late 1980s to present

Victoria Burlaka

It is logical to use 1991 as the starting point for contemporary Ukrainian art – the year the Soviet Union collapsed and Ukraine gained independence. However, the renewal of artistic language – coinciding with the euphoric zeitgeist of perestroika and glasnost (the Soviet Union's economic and political reforms of the 1980s), and the departure from the obsolete canons of socialist realism toward modern global trends – began earlier, in the late 1980s. It was then, at the all-Union exhibitions in Moscow and republic-wide exhibitions in Kyiv, that the Ukrainian New Wave movement proudly announced itself. This stylistically cohesive and aesthetically powerful collective movement lasted until about 1993; it was followed by *raskartinivanie* or 'away from painting.'

Of all the national versions of postmodern neo-expressionism, Ukrainian New Wave is most often compared to the Italian Transavantgarde, a type of 'mystery painting' in dialogue with the tradition of the medium's continuous development. While contemporaries attest that it was only books and magazines that brought the Italian Transavantgarde to Ukraine, the movement resonated with Ukrainian artists due to their deep reverence for painting. The Ukrainian version, however, was fraught with radical revisions of its meaning, form, and basic values.

Thus, the *Sorrow of Cleopatra* by Kyivans Arsen Savadov and Heorhii Senchenko exploded on the scene at the Moscow Manege exhibition of 1987, becoming a manifesto of new art and setting a unique coordinate system. Despite its heroic flourishes and style, and its emptiness of meaning, conceptually the work declared the end of the old painterly discourse. This was, in fact, the root of the artists' sorrow – while there were a wide range of quotable classics, from Velázquez to Picasso, painting would never be *real* again; it was all just a simulacrum based on the ruins of former greatness. This loving yet ironic approach was picked up by Savadov and Senchenko's younger colleagues, and inspired the spread of a new painting style in Kyiv, Odesa, and Lviv. The most notable names in this cohort were Oleksandr Hnylytskyi, Oleh Holosii, Oleksandr Roitburd, Vasyl Tsaholov, Andrii Sahaidakovskyi, Valeriia Trubina, Pavlo Kerestei, Maksym Mamsykov, Dmytro Kavsan, Serhii Panych, and Vasyl Riabchenko.

The New Wave developed into a collective movement through squatting: houses awaiting restoration in the centre of Kyiv were seized as workshops, where an active exchange of ideas and loud parties took place. The most well-known squat was on Vulytsia Paryzkoi Komuny (Paris Commune Street), which is why artists of the New Wave are often called the Paris Commune artists; likewise their eponymous exhibition curated by Oleksandr Soloviev.

The Volitional Edge of National Post-Eclecticism was a group that was both stylistically and territorially detached. It consisted of Oleh Tistol, Kostiantyn Reunov, Oleksandr Kharchenko, Maryna Skuharieva, and Yana Bystrova, among others. At the

page 216
Oleh Tistol
Reunification (detail), 1988
See Fig. 2, p. 224

turn of the decade, their version of the New Wave continued to develop in a squat in Furmanny Pereulok in Moscow, where they popularized, by their own definition, the Ukrainian version of Pop Art – Nats Art. Considering that neo-expressionism developed in Ukraine practically a decade later than elsewhere in the world, it came to an end rather quickly. The year 1992 was the last that Ukrainian artists would exist in their closed-off world: that same year, the Spielmotor Corporation invited several Paris Commune artists to a residency in Munich. In Germany, the Ukrainians had the opportunity to position themselves within the Western context of contemporary art, as presented, for example, at that year's 'documenta' (an annual German exhibition of contemporary art), where there were practically no paintings shown. The turn toward new media was already evident at the artists' final exhibition, 'Postanesthesia', at the Municipal Gallery on Lothringerstrasse.

The 1990s were a time of extreme, unconventional photo and video projects, as well as the gradual institutionalization of Ukrainian art, which was trying to establish its context by putting together disparate puzzle pieces. This centralized framework – a collective of current artists and curators, active projects and exhibitions, and the introduction of new media – was mainly associated with the Centres for Contemporary Art in Kyiv and Odesa, funded by the George Soros Open Society Foundation. In 1993 the curator Marta Kuzma came to Ukraine to become the first director of the Kyiv Soros Centre. Her own landmark projects grew out of a deep study of the Ukrainian situation – both at the time and in a historical context. This became a common feature of 1990s art: it truthfully, and sometimes painfully, reflected the harsh social realities and transformations taking place in post-Soviet society. Though at the time, art functioned in a different way from the socially critical approach that is familiar to us today, a new artistic algorithm of active, involved interaction with society, both playful and mythologized, was being developed.

Artists became explorers of dangerous marginal zones, from mines to homeless shelters. Curatorial projects similarly claimed the function of in-situ social performances. One example is *Alchemical Surrender* (1994) by Marta Kuzma, which was conceived at the height of tensions over the division of the (previously jointly owned) Black Sea Fleet between Ukraine and Russia. It took place on *Slavutych*, the flagship of the fleet. *The Crimean Project* (1998) was also directly related to the social environment. It became a reflection on the historical 'redistribution of the world' by Stalin, Churchill, and Roosevelt as a result of the 1945 Yalta Conference held in the Livadia Palace toward the close of the Second World War. In 1997, Jerzy Onuch became the director of the Centre for Contemporary Art in Kyiv. He curated a number of significant exhibitions, including 'Ukrainian Brand' (2001), in an attempt to shape a new, non-stereotypical, national identity. Beginning in the late 1990s, however, the Soros Centre's funding began to decline, unsurprisingly affecting the rhythm of artistic life.

Pavlo Makov
Fountain of
Exhaustion.
Acqua Alta, 2022
Ukrainian Pavilion
at Arsenale, Venice

The turn of the millennium and the first half of the 2000s became a time for taking stock and the first attempts at systematization and museumification of what had been produced in the field of contemporary Ukrainian art over the previous decade and a half. The most ambitious projects were carried out with the support of the Victor Pinchuk Foundation. Even before the establishment of the PinchukArtCentre in 2006 (a private institution that has since become the most authoritative and effective in terms of both supporting developing Ukrainian art and integrating it into the global context), two exhibitions were organized: 'First Collection' (2003) and 'Farewell to Arms!' (2004). These exhibitions were intended to mark the beginning of a museum of contemporary art (though subsequently, the concept of PinchukArtCentre transformed from museum to art centre), covering the most significant historical phenomena starting from the late 1980s.

New generations of artists have tended to appear during periods of historical cataclysm, along new cycles of the liberation movement and the rise of national self-consciousness in Ukraine. The 1990s generation had come together in anticipation of the USSR's imminent collapse, and dominated the art scene until the mid-2000s, when it seemed to reach a creative plateau, waiting for new ideas, people, and strategies. But then came the Orange Revolution of 2004, and yet another new generation emerged on the crest of this event. Both its way of thinking and its creative strategies were new: their art was no longer an aesthetic reflection or a mythological intervention, but a critical rethinking of what was happening in society and directly interacting with it. The Post-Orange Generation is the generation of political art. The main link in the chain of events that brought this generation to the fore was a residency at the Centre for Contemporary Art at the National University of Kyiv-Mohyla Academy (NaUKMA), offered during the Orange Maidan by Jerzy Onuch to a group of young artists. At the time, the walls of the centre became a creative laboratory, culminating in a spontaneous exhibition by the group R.E.P. (Revolutionary Experimental Space). In 2005, a similar group of young artists appeared in Kharkiv, called SOSka, consisting of Mykola Ridnyi, Bella Lohacheva, Serhii Popov, and Anna Kryventsova, who also promoted 'actionism' as the art of direct interaction with society. The reach of R.E.P. and SOSka was quite wide – their works ranged from pre-election campaigning on Maidan Nezalezhnosti (Independence Square) in the guise of a fictitious party running for parliament (see Fig. 8, p. 232) to educational activities in the form of contemporary art for a wide audience (from people who gathered on the streets of a city to villagers in the distant backwaters of the country). One of the key works of R.E.P. is the pictographic *Dictionary of Patriotism* – another attempt to determine an of-the-moment Ukrainian identity, one that was psychologically, ideologically, culturally, and historically fitting.

Specifically, it was the group R.E.P. (the permanent members of which included Nikita Kadan, Zhanna Kadyrova, Lesia Khomenko, Ksenia Hnylytska, Volodymyr Kuznietsov, and Lada Nakonechna) that determined the course of art by young Ukrainians. The difficulties facing this artistic movement's development – due to unexplored historical traumas, misunderstandings of the true mechanisms of history (the politics of history and its reinterpretation have become hot topics), and the very unclear prospects for the future (that state of uncanny limbo between yesterday and tomorrow, when the possibility of a fully-fledged today is very problematic) – became the mood of the decade. Only another outbreak of civil disobedience could shake society out of this state of stagnation. The Maidan Revolution of 2014, Russia's annexation of Crimea, the war in the Donbas – all these political events greatly influenced art. Just like society, art suffers from war and experiences *The Burn of Reality* (the name of Roman Mykhailov's installation). Naturally, this 'burn' brought to life the next generation of socio-critical art: a more subtle, closer examination of a wide range of problems and interactions through the filter of a certain melancholy and dystopia. Fittingly, the Festival of Young Artists of 2017 at the Mystetskyi Arsenal National Art and Culture Museum was titled 'The Today That Never Came' (curated by Lizaveta Herman, Maria Lanko, and Kateryna Filiuk).

Will this feeling of uncertainty change in 2022, when Ukraine is experiencing the catastrophe of war? The likely answer is yes. Old issues will fade into the background, as the war provides a new, clearer lens. On the one hand, this war brings to light the hitherto unimaginable atrocities of the enemy and the crisis of the old utopian-humanistic world order; and on the other hand, it reveals the incredible solidarity of the Ukrainian people, with their unwavering faith in victory and in new possibilities for their country.

New Wave: The Ukrainian Pictorial Transavantgarde, 1987–93

Oleksandr Roitburd's *The All-Consuming Din of Ein Sof* belongs both to the artist's own aesthetic and to the Odesa iteration of New Wave. Its allusions to and close emotional connection to all the cultural baggage of painting are characteristic of the style, which is paradoxical considering the New Wave's belief in the 'death' of fine art and the impossibility of producing true meaning and value. The author's intention was for us to see a full-blooded, pastose phantom. Roitburd paid close attention to the texture and physicality of painting, while playing with the idea of myth. The painting first appeared in 1990 at the exhibition 'Pislya modernizmu 2' (After Modernism 2) at the Odesa Museum of Fine Arts. Later, Roitburd became the museum's charismatic and effective director; he served in this role for the last three years of his life, from 2018 to 2021.

During his Transavantgarde phase, Roitburd developed the concept of a 'big picture': he ramped up the pretentiousness of the form, stretching his canvases to gigantic sizes. So, at his next exhibition, 'Novi fihuratsiyi' (New Figurations), Roitburd presented, according to the witty remark of his colleagues, a 'Berlin Wall' of paintings – an installation over sixteen metres long. The captivating quality of an apparent infinity of form (which, in fact, is only the outer shell of the void) was characteristically present in *Ein Sof*. Infinite and boundless, Ein Sof in Kabbalah philosophy is a transcendent God in the purest form; the comprehensiveness of divine thought with no limits. Motifs from Roitburd's personal iconography appear on the canvases: people as monuments, 'Adam' in the armour of a Roman soldier, 'Eve'. They balance precariously on spheres set on triangles in an abstract stormy space, against the backdrop of dense, bun-like clouds.

Having paid tribute to the genre of 'appropriation videos' popular in the 1990s, Oleksandr Roitburd remained one of the most iconic figures in Ukrainian art. After the hermeneutic phase of the New Wave movement, his artistic works became more uninhibited and reflective of what was happening at the time. The postmodern cultural dialogue – superficial and timeless, high and low, elitist and low-brow – moved toward the clarity of the meta-modern, new sincerity, and pop art, without compromising the quality of painting. Popular political and historical events and figures, past and present, were featured in art, from Hryhorii Skovoroda, Nachman of Breslov and Lenin to Yulia Tymoshenko. Such figures have smoothly transitioned from the realm of the sacred and mystical into the land of celebrities and pop idols.

Oleh Tistol, along with Kostiantyn Reunov, Oleksandr Kharchenko, Maryna Skuharieva, Yana Bystrova and Anatolii Stepanenko, created the group 'The Volitional Edge of National Post-Eclecticism' in 1988. In contrast to the universality of Roitburd's paintings, their work represented the national branch of New Wave,

1
Oleksandr Roitburd
The All-Consuming
Din of Ein Sof, 1990
Oil on canvas
400 × 300 cm
PinchukArtCentre, Kyiv

exploring the multiple facets of Ukrainian identity. Tistol was consistent in his intentions: throughout his career he adhered to the main themes he outlined at its start, such as in his *Ukrainian Money Project*, *Museum of History*, *Mountains*, and *YuBK* ('South Coast of Crimea'). He consistently advocated for the 'beauty of the national stereotype' – a version of Ukrainian pop art, its assumed ornamentality, and the reworking of iconic features and designs from everyday life. For instance, the artist was inspired by the metaphysical beauty of Soviet cigarette and cognac labels to create his mountain series, *Kazbek* and *Ararat*. An appreciation of everyday things was natural for this graduate of the faculty of Decorative and Applied Arts at the Lviv National Academy of Arts. Tistol and his compatriots often used stencils in their paintings – it was their speciality.

2
Oleh Tistol
Reunification, 1988
Oil on canvas
270 × 240 cm
PinchukArtCentre, Kyiv

Works from this period include *Reunification* (1988), *Condottiere* (1988) and *Bohdan-Zinovyi Khmelnytskyi* (1988). These works are dedicated to using the lens of postmodern irony to rethink the national myth about the supposed 'reunification' of Ukraine with Russia in 1654. Allegedly, Hetman Bohdan Khmelnytskyi petitioned to Tsar Alexei for help, citing religious and social oppression of the Orthodox population by the Polish–Lithuanian Commonwealth, and so the Zaporizhzhian army and the territories of the Hetmanate under its control voluntarily submitted to Russian rule (see chapter 4). The story behind this 'reunification' and the preceding Pereiaslav Agreement, at which a historic decision was made by Cossack commanders, was very popular in Soviet art. Just take a look at *Forever with Moscow, Forever with the Russian People* by Mykhailo Khmelko, to better understand this tale. Perhaps Tistol was referencing the full spectrum of works on this topic all at once, implying that Ukraine, falling into the patronizing grip of Russia, would sooner or later regret it. Today, his work's hidden subtext is obvious.

Oleh Holosii was the last romantic of the New Wave generation. He passed away tragically early in 1993, at the age of twenty-eight. Following his death, the New Wave movement came to its logical conclusion. As was seen in a retrospective exhibition in 2019 at the Mystetskyi Arsenal, Holosii was a brilliant, intuitive visionary painter. He could see other worlds and dimensions – from the darkest to the brightest – and the legacy he left behind would be enough for many. According to the memoirs of his partner Valeriia Trubina, he painted with lightning speed, in a single impulse – a picture in a night. His work is clearly divided into two periods. First, the heroic Transavantgarde, when he absorbed the great tradition of museum paintings, from Piero della Francesca to Francis Bacon, from Konstantin Makovsky to Giorgio de Chirico. Art historian Ekaterina Degot called his next period of post-media filmmaking 'Gifts of a Kleptomaniac': a shameless appropriation of anything that caught the artist's eye, most often spectacular shots of classic films. According to his colleagues, Holosii once bought a book called *Hollywood* at a market, and then redrew it in its entirety. *Good* (1991) was also a film snapshot from his inner world – a representation of the artist's psychedelic trance, a state of oneness with the world that few experience. It shows a panorama of a fiery sunset on a tropical island, and then the air thickens, becoming alive, visible, and pulsing, as the flight paths of flies with human faces cut trenches in the air. One fly, hovering in a state of bliss, is endowed with the face of the artist, revealing the artist's insight into the meaning of life: to simply exist.

Oleh Holosii
Good, 1991
Oil on canvas
200 × 300 cm
PinchukArtCentre, Kyiv

Art of the 1990s: The Development of Staged Photography and Video, 1993–2001

Arsen Savadov largely determined the trajectory and style of Ukrainian art from the late 1980s through the 2000s. It is no exaggeration to say that he is one of the central figures in Ukrainian art. *Cleopatra's Sorrow* (1987) and later *Vital Season* (1987) and *Melancholia* (1988; co-authored with Heorhii Senchenko) became the starting points of the Ukrainian Transavantgarde. These works were icons of style, forming an epic canon and influencing a circle of artists around him.

In the 1990s, when artists began to depart from painting as a practice, Savadov continued to hold one of the central roles in the art world due to his ability to clearly conceptualize and embody his message in an ambitious, large-scale manner. From 1997 until the mid-2000s, photo projects sprouted one after another: *Donbas-Chocolate* (1997), *Fashion at the Graveyard* (1997), *Collective Red* (1998–99), *Angels* (1997–98), *Underground 2000* (1999), *Kokto* (2001), *Book of the Dead* (2001), and *Last Project* (2002). Savadov calls these social performances, or social documents. We are not talking about documentary photography, however, but rather about intervention, infiltration into the heart of society, and about interacting with it in dangerous marginal zones (art, itself, is one such marginal zone) such as mines, meat processing plants, cemeteries, and even morgues.

There are many stories about how the spectacle of art unfolds in extreme environments. Savadov has talked about how his photoshoots turned into initiation rituals: in one, an enthusiastic photography crew was 'lowered into the lava' of the hot hell of a mine ('our balls stuck in our throats'). Once these 'newcomers' made friends with the miners, the men willingly posed for photos in incongruous ballet tutus, as if they were creatures not of this world (Fig. 4). According to the artist, the turbulent 1990s were a cynical time when humanistic values became devalued; it was a period that required an adequate means of self-expression, not trivializing what was happening, but grasping at its essence, excavating it as if with a scalpel. This head-on collision of ethics and aesthetics culminated in photos in the spirit of Caravaggio, composed of dead bodies at a morgue: the viewer does not immediately understand who or what they are looking at. For all the harshness of the spectacle, while putting the image together, Savadov remained entirely an aesthete and transmedia artist. His photo series are full of pictorial allusions to fine art, and follow the laws of composition; his subsequent paintings – he returned to painting at the beginning of the 2000s, when times were calmer – were composed of materials from his photo shoots.

The idea of 'pseudo-documentarism' – fictitious, but more convincing than ordinary reality – was developed by Vasyl Tsaholov, a connoisseur of 'criminal

4
Arsen Savadov
From the series
***Donbas-Chocolate*, 1997**
Colour print
180 × 120 cm
PinchukArtCentre

5
Illya Chychkan
From the series *Sleeping Princes*
***of Ukraine,* 1997**
30 × 20 cm
PinchukArtCentre

romance'. According to him, the only convincing photos are those that were deliberately staged. Alongside sky-rocketing crime statistics, the 1990s were also a time of great interest in the films of Quentin Tarantino – indeed, scenes like those in *Pulp Fiction* existed in both life and art. Tsaholov's performances and installations were similarly characterized by interventions in the social environment. In *Karl Marx – Père Lachaise* (1993) members of the art scene were theatrically 'shot' in broad daylight in the centre of Kyiv; in *Bandit Skirmish* (2000) in Bratislava, cars containing 'dead' mannequins were planted throughout the city. *Criminal Week* (1994), *Soft Horrors* (1998), and, finally, a narrative video about a maniacal psychoanalyst fascinated by magic, *Milk Sausages* (1998), are all from the same body of works reflecting on the effect of staged violence.

The staged photos and videos of these times gravitated toward shocking aesthetics, but were, in the end, the quintessence of reality itself. *Sleeping Princes of Ukraine* (1997) by Illya Chychkan shows abnormal embryos from an anatomical museum, which the artist adorned with flashy jewelry. It was a spectacle in the spirit of camp, as well as an allusion to the consequences of the Chornobyl disaster. Together with Piotr Wyrzykowski, Chychkan created the dystopian photo-video project *Atomic Love* (2001), in which 'the last people', dressed in protective suits and spacesuits, walk along the deserted landscape of the Chornobyl exclusion zone; they kiss and make love. Eighteen years later (in collaboration with Ihor Tyshchenko), Chychkan returned to this subject matter in his now-famous theatrical character of a man-monkey. *51 2763° N, 30 2219° E* is the geolocation of Prypiat, Ukraine (one of the towns evacuated after the Chornobyl nuclear disaster), and in this video it has become a land without a name: a ghost town where there are no longer people, but where a 'mutant' frolics in the form of a large monkey.

Another radical gesture, another circle of hell – a dangerous trip behind the looking glass of society that must be mentioned when speaking of the uncompromising spirit of this decade – is the series *Case History* (2001) by Borys Mykhailov, shown by curator Jerzy Onuch at the Centre for Contemporary Art at NaUKMA. Visiting the Kharkiv homeless – a far from safe undertaking, since Mykhailov's approach not only lacked good manners, but also even a basic understanding of acceptable forms of social behaviour – Mykhailov asked these people to undress and reveal their bodies, mutilated by diseases. His work transformed their bodily sores into the mental sores of a society sick with indifference. And why was this necessary? Probably because – as the artist never tires of repeating – beauty is truth.

'The 1990s were also a time of great interest in the films of Quentin Tarantino – indeed, scenes like those in *Pulp Fiction* existed in both life and art.'

Political Art of the Post-Orange Generation, 2004–14

The generation that came of age in the mid-noughties was radically different from its predecessors in terms of its members' vision of art's objectives and their methods of realization. Tiberii Silvashi (who first appeared on the art scene in the 1980s) once described the worldview of the 2000s generation as more 'effective than affective,' meaning that rational political messages, and the distinct language of their transmission, were better understood by the Western art system. So, in addition to an internal need for critical expression that was especially ripe at that time in Ukrainian art, Post-Orange artists also took into account the fact that politics and art were one and the same.

Nikita Kadan is one of the undisputed leaders of this generation. He was a member of the R.E.P. group (see Fig. 8, p. 232), which became a successful springboard for the individual careers of all its members. Starting with his 2009 project *Procedure Room*, in which white, imperial Soviet-style plates were printed with drawings of various methods of police torture recorded by human rights activists, Kadan's commentary on the system is clearly critical. Kadan developed a characteristic way of reflecting time and ideology in one another: today is always seen through the perspective or prism of yesterday. Kadan is keenly interested in the politics of history, which is never objective but always interpreted from one subjective point of view or another. In his graphic series of black-and-white drawings, *Pogrom* (2016–17), Kadan references photographs taken during the Jewish pogrom in Lviv in July 1941, in which thousands of Jewish

6
Zhanna Kadyrova
'Security Cameras' from
***Invisible Forms*, 2015**
Wood, cement
Installation view, Cent Quatre,
Paris, France

7
Nikita Kadan
The Little House of the Giants,
2012
Found objects, wood, metal,
gypsum, paint
Installation view,
PinchukArtCentre

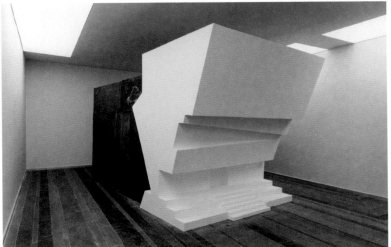

people were killed, and many more forced out of their homes and publicly humiliated. He addresses the problem of the manipulation of historical memory and its (mis)interpretation for the purposes of propaganda. For Kadan, there is no 'objective truth', but rather, history is an interweaving of many historical, national, and personal interests. Kadan's 2021 retrospective exhibition at the PinchukArtCentre 'Stone Beats Stone' embodied the artist's interest in historical revisionism and Kadan's post-utopian, post-avant-garde vision. *The Little House of the Giants* (2012) is one of his hybrid works, consisting of a dissonance of high and low notes; in this case, an ugly, 1970s Soviet bunk house is fused with the clean forms of an ideal architectural object in the style of Soviet neo-modernism. It speaks of grotesque exaggeration:

the idealization of the proletariat's role in both Soviet architecture and art, as well as in the ideology that gave rise to them.

Zhanna Kadyrova, who developed the pop-art idea of an anti-monument to ordinary invisible things, similarly reflects on the tangible embodiment of historical memory. Kadyrova recycled materials from everyday life: she used old Soviet tiles from the walls of buildings vanishing into the past to construct new things, thus giving the past a second life. Kadyrova's series *Invisible Forms* (Fig. 6, p. 230), shown in full in 2011 at the Mystetskyi Arsenal, was an attempt to revolutionize our vision of reality. We are accustomed to the fact that sculpture immortalizes not just the obvious, but the exaggerated. It presents and draws attention to the work in an empty space, but disregards the empty space itself; although the world, for the most part, consists of such space. The distance from the nucleus of an atom to its electron is many times greater than its size – therefore, the world practically sinks in emptiness, and, Kadyrova suggests, we are constantly 'falling through' it. Kadyrova presents this idea in complete visual clarity as she gives shape to the beams of light from lanterns, spotlights, projectors, and surveillance cameras. These intangible, invisible 'things' are embodied in their very antipode, in the most brutal and substantial of all possible materials: concrete.

A 3D copy of Kadyrova's *Monument to the Monument* (a monument-shaped object under a veil), installed in Sharhorod, became both the figurative and actual title of the national Ukrainian project shown at the Venice Biennale in 2013. At the time, the subject of decommunization and the dismantling of Soviet monuments was especially topical. A monument – according to the very etymology of the word – is a concentrated, material embodiment of historical and cultural memory. The

8
R.E.P. Group
We Will R.E.P. You, **2005**
Maidan Nezalezhnosti, Kyiv

9
Stas Voliazlovskyi
The Feat of the Matroskin Horse,
2015
Textile, ballpoint pen, mixed media
136 × 161 cm
From the collection of Boris
and Tatyana Grinev

manipulation of history and its endless rewriting destroys our sense of reality – both what once happened and what is happening today. The horrible tradition of starting a new historical cycle by completely razing the old to the ground was characteristic of Soviet times. Part of that same 2013 Venice Biennale project was Mykola Ridnyi's video *Monument* (2012), which showed, from the supposedly detached position of an observer, the dramatic destruction of the utopia of the past. The recording showed the dismantling of a Soviet monument in Kharkiv and the installation of a new one.

The Orange Revolution and the Maidan Revolution intensified awareness of the social context, perhaps best exemplified in the public performance works by experimental artist group R.E.P., of which both Kadan and Khadyrova are members. *We Will R.E.P. You* took place on 7 November, 2005, when two demonstrations – by communists and nationalists – were held in the politically-charged arena of Kyiv's Maidan Nezalezhnosti (Independence Square). The artists 'led' these crowds of demonstrators, performing as a independent political group with banners quoting Andy Warhol and Joseph Beuys.

Another result of the political and social intensification awareness in art was the rise of Stas Voliazlovskyi's 'Chanson Art'. Voliazlovskyi created vibrant and unique versions of his own type of ethnographic art: ballpoint-pen drawings on textiles or on paper in the form of placard newspapers, reminiscent of labour camp tattoos (Fig. 9). Commenting on his creative style, the artist, either jokingly or seriously, endorsed 'chanson radio' – music that can be heard on every city minibus, that plagues the 'high-brow' segment of the population, and is considered both a vestige of Soviet culture and a marker of provincial existence.

Postmedia Painting: 2000s

Oleksandr Hnylytskyi was a prominent representative of Transavantgarde painting of the Ukrainian New Wave in the late 1980s and early 1990s. It was he who largely determined its specific, fascinating features, such as 'childish discourse' or 'cute-ism', or making abrupt, incomplete statements. In order, no doubt, to 'kill off' painting, he produced works reminiscent of children's drawings in huge formats. Tetiana Yablonska, a famous socialist realist painter, fainted when she saw Hnylytskyi's painting *The Call of Laodicea on the Lycus*. The goal of disrupting the foundations of art was achieved on a nihilistic level of youthful maximalism, and the artist would later return to this medium with a new understanding of its objectives.

From 2005 until his death in 2009, Hnylytskyi painted in the manner of illusionism. Normally a style that fits within the definition of photorealism, Hnylytskyi's version did not gravitate toward photographic detail at all. By completely generalizing the image, he created a vivid illusion of an object in space, unfolding a kind of 'theatre of the object.' Hnylytskyi's work is dominated by resounding silence and metaphysicality. His true heroes are chairs, chandeliers, lamps, doors, windows, and flights of stairs persistently leading the audience into another dimension. The first project of this kind was *Dacha* (2005), displayed at the TSEKH Gallery in Kyiv. The artist employed a style of deception – in which the image and the object are indistinguishable – that originated in the Netherlands in the seventeenth century. Painted images replaced the rubbish that filled a garage: a red motorcycle, refrigerators, books. This was his commentary on the unnecessary items that are a pity to throw away: people are bound to all this junk through sentimental affection, because things are avatars moving ahead of us into non-existence.

For artists, every object they depict becomes an alter ego. A person is reflected in the object, and the object in the person – both literally and figuratively. Hnylytskyi inherited his love of reflective surfaces from traditional photorealism. The flash in *Chocolate Factory* (2009) is a symbol for the artist's existential insights. It appears – a romantic stormy light – against the dark-grey background of the sky. This is undoubtably both an artistic device and a self-portrait, so evident is the emotional connection between the artist and the image as object.

Vasyl Tsaholov also began his journey in the late 1980s, and with his seven-metre-long canvas *Leviathan* he set the course of Ukrainian New Wave art. Soon after, in 1992, he created the figurative series *The Rubber of Feelings*, paintings that resemble stills from action movies. This brings forth the style of postmedia: when one medium inherits the specifics of another. (As previously mentioned, Tsaholov, in his performance, photo, and video works of the 1990s, adhered to the genre of criminal poetics.) Postmedia came into being with *The Rubber of Feelings*, which has it all: the subtle melancholy of non-existence and the unrestrained spectacle of violence. It also shows the artist's clear position – which Tsaholov would further develop in

10
Oleksandr Hnylytskyi
Chocolate Factory, **2009**
Oil on canvas
304 × 214 cm

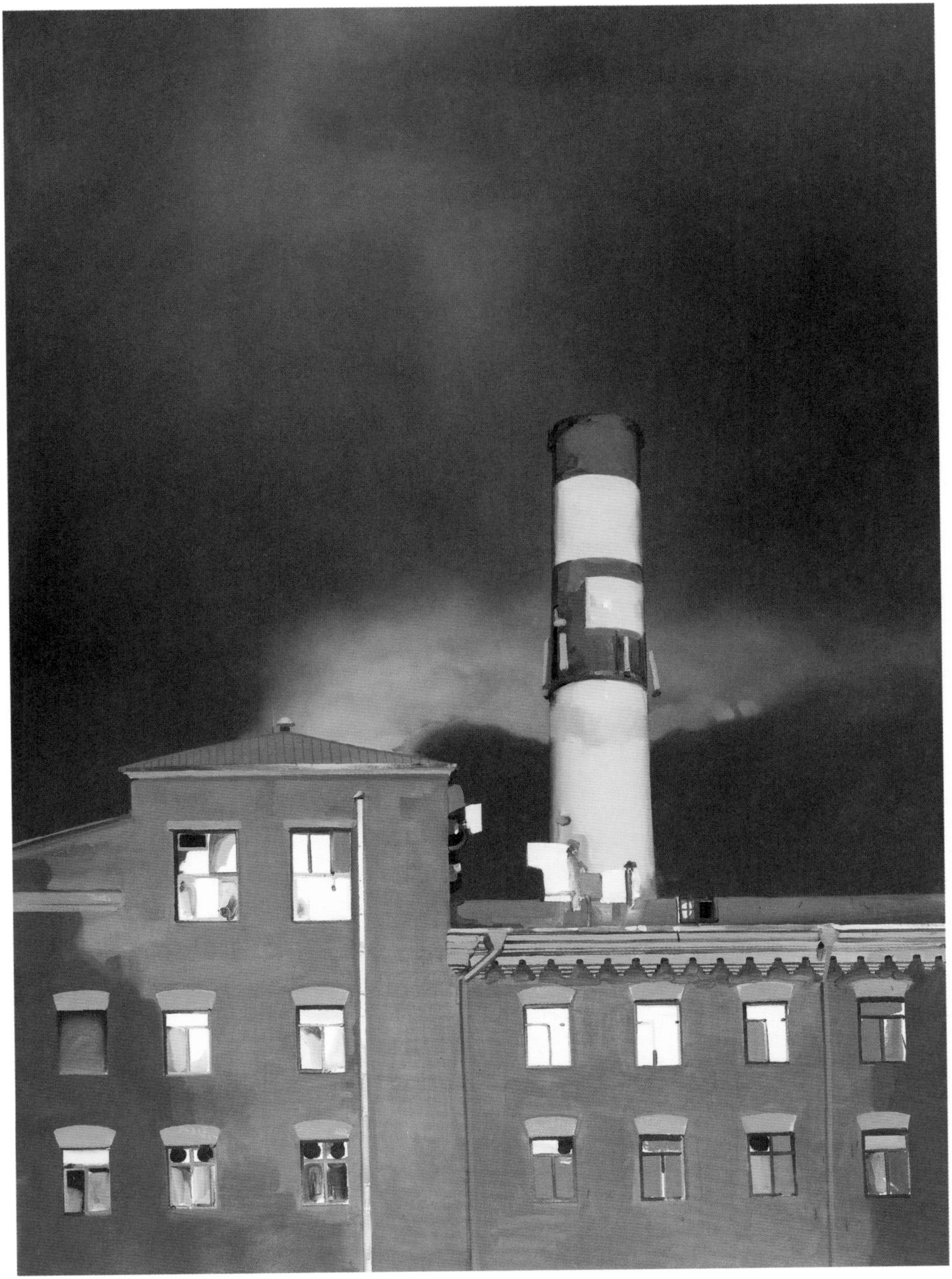

11
Vasyl Tsaholov
Fly, 2012
From the series *Phantoms of Fear*
Oil on canvas
280 × 380 cm

12 (*opposite*)
Tiberii Silvashi
Painting, 2000
Acrylic, water, wood, cellophane
Installation view, Centre for
Contemporary Art at the
Kyiv-Mohyla Academy

the future – which was one of a cold distancing between the manner of painting and the one undertaking it. Tsaholov, as it were, pours out onto the canvas some of the unfiltered flow of information that surrounds him; there is nothing personal there.

In the early 2000s, this distancing of the artist from himself creates gaps in his visual field, which is covered with blanks or blind spots. The flatness of the canvas resembles the flickering of a television screen – the information matrix of everyday life. The external corresponds to the internal, as Tsaholov began working with themes of ironically transformed anecdotal mass-media stories, such as the invasion of fields and pigsties by aliens in *Ukrainian X-File* (2001). One after another, he produced works that exploited the phobias of the masses: *Phantoms of Fear* (2002), *A Bandit's Bullet* (2005), *Who Does Hirst Fear?* (2009), and *Fear Has Big Eyes* (2014). At the top of the pyramid of human fears remains the fear of terrorism, which the artist sometimes discusses in an Aesopian manner. A giant *Fly* (2012) – a green monster in an explosive belt against the backdrop of a bloody sunset – evokes a shiver of horror and disgust. *O tempora, o mores!*: times may change, but customs remain forever bloodthirsty.

Along with figurative painting in all its forms, abstraction has been developing in Ukrainian art from the early 1990s to the present day. It has evolved in line with the Modernist aesthetic discourse, defending the autonomy of plastic values as a kind of neoplasticism. The Kyiv exhibition 'Pictorial Reserve' in 1992, in which Tiberii Silvashi, Mark Geiko, Anatolii Kryvolap, and Oleksandr Zhyvotkov took part, served as a starting point. This trend in non-narrative art took place alongside radical reductionism, resulting in so-called non-objective art. In 2017, the group Kyiv Non-Objective (KNO) was formed, and included Silvashi, Badri Gubianuri, Yelena Dombrovska, Miroslav Vaida, and Serhii Popov. According to Silvashi, the group's ideologue, such art is the only truth in a world of post-truth, as it does not impose any meanings or associations on viewers, but forces them to delve deeper into themselves.

The 2000 project *Painting* at the Centre for Contemporary Art at NaUKMA was conceived by curator Jerzy Onuch as a dialogue between two significant abstract artists – Tiberii Silvashi (with assistants Ilona Silvashi, Yaroslav Prysiazhniuk, and Yurii Ermolenko) and the Polish artist Leon Tarasewicz – about the modern role and functions of painting. This project became the next stage of Silvashi's reflections on the fact that colour and its material carrier – paint – can themselves become the main subject of a painting. By creating a space of total colour, the artist immerses the viewer entirely within it, giving us the opportunity to enter the painting.

A New Social Turn: Art of the 2010s and Early 2020s

Each new round of the liberation movement in Ukraine gives impetus to action for a new generation of artists. The Maidan Revolution of 2014, the occupation of Crimea and the Donbas, and the war with Russia in 2022 (which has in fact been ongoing since 2014) – each inevitably changed the configuration of the art scene, in which a wave of social transformations associated with the new realities of war is clearly visible. Political art is still the main trend, and it continues to develop and evolve. The degree of explicitly politically-charged work has decreased, and in its place are greater depth, poetry, and a certain anthropological approach: artists are closely studying the specific aspects of existence here and now, and the intersections of politics, history, and culture.

The revolution of 2014 not only gave rise to new generations of artists, but also gave new meanings to the work of well-known artists of older generations. One example is Vlada Ralko, who created the grandiose graphic series *Kyiv Diary* (featuring more than 400 works on A4-sized paper). The series is packed with the emotions evoked in us by what was happening at the time – from the joy of national pride to the depths of despair. And we continue to experience such emotions: Ralko is already creating a new chronicle about the current war. In her *Lviv Diary* she broadcasts not only the daily content of the horrors of the war, but also the resilience and the good that she discovers in people. That is to say, she is interested in people's humanity, which difficult historical times tend to reveal.

This new stage of critical art is distinctly characterized by its focus on problems that affect the new generation, and works that explore such themes are often nominated for the Pinchuk Art Prize. The development of such historical discourse (if not objective, then at least demonstrating its conditionality) has already been discussed. Hot topics include the changing concepts of gender identity and gender roles, the post-Soviet collective consciousness and unconscious, war, and the crisis of anthropocentrism and all its ensuing consequences. The establishment of the PinchukArtCentre awards for young artists (the national and international Future Generation prize) contributed much to the development of young artists and art in Ukraine. This new generation of artists has not come to the fore this decade by chance – they are the ones who most readily reflect the catastrophic transformations of our reality. The work featured at the Festival of Young Artists at the Mystetskyi Arsenal (2017) and the Second Kharkiv Biennial of Young Art (2019) confirmed this.

Roman Khimei and Yarema Malashchuk are two representative figures of the new Ukrainian art scene. Their work demonstrates a notable turn to the screen – right now, video as a medium is becoming especially popular. Hailing from Kolomyia, they studied at the Institute of Screen Arts of the Kyiv National University of Cinema,

13
Vlada Ralko
From the series *Kyiv Diary*, **2014**
Paper, watercolour, mixed media
30 × 20 cm

Theatre, and Television. Since 2013, they have been working together at the cutting edge of visual art and cinema, as artists, camera operators, and directors. Their videos are idiosyncratic diagnoses of certain social strata: in their own words, they 'speak of social groups and communities' that testify to the state of public consciousness as a whole. The artists work in the genre of mockumentary – pseudo-documentary films. While they appear to be casually watching what is happening, they are actually exploring the possibilities of artistically designing a scene. In 2018, they received the second Pinchuk Art Prize for their film *To Whom Have You Abandoned Us, Our Father!* (Fig. 14, p. 240); in 2019 they received the first prize of the MUHI competition (Young

239

Ukrainian Artists Prize) for their film *Dedicated to the Youth of the World*; and in 2020, they were the main winners of the Pinchuk Art Prize for their film *Live Broadcast*. The film's title explains their approach to interacting with reality: the artists appear to be broadcasting live while witnessing strange scenes, when in reality, they are producing a staged show. In *To Whom Have You Abandoned Us…* (2018) Khimei and Malashchuk recreated a rehearsal of the Chernihiv Regional Philharmonic Choir, who performed as the townspeople from Modest Mussorgsky's Russian opera *Boris Godunov*. This production, simultaneously ordinary and sublime, clearly conveys the ingrained Soviet mentality and entropy that still reigns in our official institutions – cultural and otherwise. This work makes it possible to talk about young artists' work as passéistic criticism, reflecting the present through the prism of the legacy of the past.

Kharkiv artists Danyyl Revkovskyi and Andrii Rachynskyi work in the same field of analysing marginal niches and factions, leading to an unfavourable diagnosis of society as a whole. At the 2018 Pinchuk Art Prize nominee exhibition, they presented a work in the spirit of investigative journalism, with photos taken from social networks and urban environments. They focused on the tragedy that occurred in 1996 in the city of Dniprodzerzhynsk (now Kamianske), when the KTM-5 tram suffered a brake system failure, which led to the death of thirty-four people and injured more than one hundred. In 2021, the artists put on a solo exhibition at the PinchukArtCentre called 'Tailings Dam', representing a future Museum of Human Civilization, supposedly created after its demise. It addresses the archaeology of a complex of special facilities intended for the storage of radioactive and toxic waste from mineral processing in Kryvyi Rih. This dystopian vision shows where humanity's barbaric treatment of

14
**Yarema Malashchuk
and Roman Khimei**
***To Whom Have You Abandoned
Us, Our Father!*, 2018**

Earth's resources could soon lead. The most impactful part of the work is a video in which the artists have grown accustomed to being the 'last people' on Earth.

What does the future of contemporary art hold for Ukraine? At the time of publication, the country remains at war following the Russian invasion of February 2022. To date, at least 250 museums and galleries in Ukraine have been destroyed or damaged by Russian forces, and precious artefacts, including Scythian gold, have been stolen or looted. Nevertheless, support for Ukraine in the wider art world is heartening. In April 2022, Pavlo Makov left a bomb shelter in Kharkiv to represent Ukraine at the Venice Biennale (see p. 220); another exhibition, 'This Is Ukraine', created in partnership with the Office of the President, showcased works by both contemporary and historical Ukrainian artists, alongside pieces by international artists created in solidarity. The Shadows Project, meanwhile, continues to campaign for artists and artworks previously categorized as Russian to have their heritage acknowledged at last: as a result, the National Gallery in London finally changed the title of a Degas painting from *Russian Dancers* to *Ukrainian Dancers*. And the country itself holds strong: precious artefacts and masterpieces of Ukrainian art have been moved to secure storage; curators and artists have been evacuated; and monuments are piled high with protective sandbags. On 10 June 2022, Kyiv's Mystetskyi Arsenal opened a new show – the first since the beginning of the war – titled 'An Exhibition About Our Feelings', exploring how the Ukrainian perception of art has changed in recent months. The exhibition text encapsulates the country's spirit of resilience: 'Pain and shock do not exhaust our lives. There is also hope, persistence, devotion, love. There still is beauty, and there is [a] future.'

15
**Danyyl Revkovskyi
and Andrii Rachynskyi**
Tailings Dam, 2020

Folk Art

by Alisa Lozhkina

Where did art first originate? Certainly not in academies, museums, and galleries. The institutional structure of art is a product of the relatively recent past, having developed over the last few centuries. But the desire to create is inherent, and not only in professional artists. Folk art is a significant component of the world's artistic heritage. Moreover, the very division of art into professional and folk – 'high' art and applied art, insiders and outsiders – is artificial. Professional art represents just one of the stages in the history of art, in a particular part of the globe.

Ukrainian folk art is a mix of traditions rooted both in antiquity and more modern developments. On the one hand, it seems to be frozen in time, following a set of codes and conventions from a bygone era. On the other, folk art is surprisingly adaptable, incorporating new technologies, materials, and even changing cultural values. Over centuries, Ukrainian folk art developed in parallel with fine art. In fact, it served the cultural needs of the majority of the population, since before the advent of mass reproduction and the spread of literacy, fine art was available only to the elite.

Folk-art objects often have both artistic and practical value, although this is not always the case. Occupying a space that is somewhere between utilitarian and purely decorative art is the icon: an indispensable item in any Ukrainian home. In rural huts, icons were traditionally displayed in the 'red corner' – a specially designated place for them, bedecked in embroidered towels called *rushnyki*. Meanwhile, artworks including painted murals on hut walls, folk easel oil paintings, and decorated Easter eggs had a predominantly aesthetic function. One of the most common subjects of Ukrainian folk paintings was the image of the Cossack Mamai (a Ukrainian folk hero), depicted sitting in the middle of the steppe holding a traditional Ukrainian instrument, a bandura. In the nineteenth and early twentieth centuries, paintings of everyday subjects became quite common, mainly idyllic landscapes and floral compositions. This art of the 'silent majority' is magnetic – not just due to its archetypal nature, but also because of the feeling of happiness that dominates most of the paintings. It may appear that the euphoric world captured in folk painting is representative of simpler times, perpetuating a whimsical myth about the golden age of folk art existing in some sort of Ukrainian utopia. However, it should be remembered that the idealistic optimism of folk paintings acts as a kind of strategy of psychological protection from the burdens of everyday life. The harder life is, the greater the desire for idyll.

Among the most interesting types of Ukrainian folk art are hand-decorated, wax-resist Easter eggs called *pysanky*. The tradition is rooted in pre-Christian spring rites associated with the awakening of nature and the cult of fertility. In Ukrainian Christian culture, *pysanky* have long been a ubiquitous feature of the Easter holidays. Modern *pysanky* were preceded by *krashanky* – eggs that were uniformly dyed in a single colour – and later *krapanky* – eggs dyed with one colour at a time, on top of which droplets of wax were evenly applied. The same technique of using wax to decorate eggs is used for *pysanky*, except that the wax is not dripped onto the egg directly but administered with a special stylus. *Pysanka* decoration is difficult to systematize due to the huge number of designs and motifs. Traditionally, all eggs were coloured with natural dyes made from plant or animal matter.

Until 1861, peasants produced decorative and applied arts not only for personal use, but also as tribute for their landowners. For example, according to historical documents from 1834, a serf master potter was required to produce 10,400 clay tiles and 15,600 pots per year in exchange for meagre wages. Meanwhile, potters also had to work in the fields in order to grow crops to feed their families. After the abolition of serfdom, the payment for handiwork remained low, but craftsmen began to focus more on selling their wares at markets.

Eventually, in places where folk art was especially widespread, handicraft trades thrived and certain towns became known as regional centres of folk art and crafts, some still to this day. Reshetylivka (Poltava oblast) and Dihtiari (Chernihiv oblast) grew into major suppliers of carpets, fabrics, and embroideries; Krolevets (Sumy oblast) developed a name for its characteristic red-and-white woven towels; and Opishnia (Poltava oblast) and Bubnivka (Vinnytsia oblast) supplied high-quality ceramic tableware and decorative clay products. In the west of Ukraine, the largest centre of traditional arts and crafts was the city of Kosiv (Ivano-Frankivsk oblast), best known for its ceramics – especially the production of ceramic stove tiles, famous for their simple yet expressive images and recognizable beige and green colour scheme. In Crimea, in the south of the country, the decorative arts of the Crimean Tatars actively developed. One of the characteristic features of the art of this region is the embellishment of various household items with traditional Ornek ornamentation.

In Soviet times, specialized factories were opened for production in many of the cities noted for their folk crafts. Their work was widely admired, not only in Ukraine and other republics of the USSR, but also abroad, where Ukrainian folk art received a number of accolades at specialized exhibitions. After the collapse of the USSR, production was mainly continued by individual artist-entrepreneurs.

Among the various forms of folk art, a special place is occupied by weaving, embroidery, and other methods of producing and embellishing fabric. Perhaps the most famous – a symbol of the country and its traditional culture – is the Ukrainian women's and men's embroidered shirt, the *vyshyvanka*. Historically, Ukrainian costume combined characteristic Slavic decorations and elements of design that came to Ukraine from the Eurasian steppe. Ukrainian traditional costumes have significant regional differences; sometimes on the two banks of the same river, people had completely different stylistic preferences.

Ukrainian folk art is distinguished by its special attention to colour. Preference is given to bright colours that have the strongest emotional impact. No less impressive are the purely geometric patterns. At the beginning of the twentieth century, innovative artists actively engaged with folk traditions. The aesthetics of Ukrainian folk art made a strong impression on Oleksandra Ekster, Kazimir Malevich, and other avant-garde artists. Bright abstract fabrics, embroidery, and especially icons and *pysanka* eggs are familiar and invaluable examples of art created not on the basis of realist principles, but grounded in rhythm, colour, and frequently, magical fantasy.

Among the most interesting types of Ukrainian folk art are hand-decorated, wax-resist Easter eggs called pysanky. Eggs are dyed with one colour at a time, on top of which droplets of wax are evenly applied using a special stylus.

The tradition is rooted in pre-Christian spring rites associated with the awakening of nature and the cult of fertility. In Ukrainian Christian culture, pysanky have long been a ubiquitous feature of the Easter holidays. See page 242.

245

Chronology

c. 45,000 BCE	c. 5500–2750 BCE	c. 10th century BCE	7th–3rd century BCE	c. 6th century BCE	422 BCE	3rd century BCE
First Neanderthal settlers.	Trypillian culture flourishes during the Neolithic and Bronze Age.	Nomadic Cimmerians settle in region of southern Ukraine.	Scythian tribes control the steppes of southern Ukraine.	Ancient Greek city-states established on the northern Black Sea coast.	The ancient Greek city-state of Chersonesus established in present-day Sevastopol.	Sarmatian tribes conquer the Scythians in Crimea.

1240	1349	1362	1370s	1397	1439	1453
Sack of Kyivan Rus by Mongols; eastern regions absorbed into Mongol Golden Horde.	Poland gains control of Lviv.	Battle of Blue Waters: the Golden Horde loses its right to collect tribute from lands between the Baltic and the Black Sea.	Armenian Cathedral built in Lviv.	Kyiv Psalter produced.	Lviv Dormition Brotherhood founded.	Fall of Constantinople.

1580–81	1615	1648	1654	1686	1687	c. 1700–60
Publication of Ostroh Bible.	Confraternal school, later the Kyiv-Mohyla Academy, is founded in Kyiv.	Cossack rebellion against the Polish–Lithuanian Commonwealth, led by Bohdan Khmelnytskyi.	Cossack Hetmanate is formed. Treaty of Pereiaslav puts Ukrainian lands under control of the Russian Empire.	The region east of the Dnipro River comes under Russian rule.	Ivan Mazepa becomes Hetman of the Cossack state.	Life of Rabbi Israel ben Eliezer (the Besht), founder of Hasidism, in Medzhybizh.

1814	1853–56	1855	1861	1863	1865	1869
Birth of poet and artist Taras Shevchenko.	The Crimean War is fought between Russia and an alliance of France, the Ottoman Empire, the UK and Piedmont-Sardinia.	Siege of Sevastopol.	The first railway opens in Ukraine; serfdom is abolished in the Russian Empire; Taras Shevchenko dies.	The Valuev Circular, a secret decree by the Russian Empire, forbids publications in the Ukrainian language.	Odesa Art School, the oldest art school in the country, was founded as a 'drawing school'.	First private school of drawing and painting in the Russian Empire opens in Kharkiv.

1917	1917	1917–19: THE SOVIET-UKRAINIAN WAR				1919–21
Foundation of the Ukrainian Academy of Art.	Russian Revolution.	1917–18	1917	1918	1918–19	The Polish–Soviet War.
		Bolshevik uprisings.	The capital of the Ukrainian Soviet Republic is moved to Kharkiv.	The Central Council of Ukraine proclaims the Ukrainian People's Republic a sovereign state.	Civil war in Ukraine; invasion of the Red Army; anti-Soviet uprisings.	

1959	1964	1972	1986	1990	1991	1992
Stepan Bandera killed by KGB in Munich.	Artists Valentyn Khrushch and Stanislav Sychov's guerrilla exhibition at the Palais-Royal Garden in Odesa.	Artist group Vremia formed in Kharkiv.	Chornobyl nuclear disaster.	400,000 Ukrainians form a human chain from Lviv to Kyiv as a demonstration of the country's desire for independence.	Fall of Soviet Union; over 90% of Ukrainians vote for independence.	Leonid Kuchma is elected Prime Minister.

2006	2006	2008	2010	2011	2012	2013
Moscow cuts off gas supplies to Ukraine.	PinchukArtCentre established in Kyiv.	Yuschenko and then-prime minister Yulia Tymoshenko request membership action plan for joining NATO.	Yanukovych is elected president.	Opposition leader Tymoshenko is jailed; more than 100 people are killed during violence between police and protesters.	Ukraine hosts the Euro 2012 football championship with Poland; many European countries boycott matches due to Tymoshenko's mistreatment in prison.	Yanukovych refuses to sign Association Agreement with the EU; Maidan protests break out, calling for his resignation.

Coloured squares indicate chapters covering each time period.

■ 47 BCE	■ 3ʳᵈ–4ᵗʰ century CE	■ 5ᵗʰ–7ᵗʰ century CE	■ 9ᵗʰ century CE	■ 988	■ 1222	■ 1230s
Crimean Peninsula under control of Roman Empire.	Ostrogoths and Huns invade and displace the power of the Scythians, Sarmatians, and Romans.	Various groups and tribes expand over Ukrainian lands, including Khazars, Slavic tribes, the Antes people, and Bulgars.	Emergence of the kingdom of Kyivan Rus.	Volodymyr the Great adopts Orthodox Christianity.	Pope Honorius III orders the closing of Orthodox churches, leads to Latin Crusades in Rus.	First Mongol invasions of Rus.

■ 1458	■ 1475	■ Late 15ᵗʰ century	■ 1514	■ 1532	■ 1552	■ 1569
Vilnius Kushnirski Brotherhood founded.	The Crimean Khanate becomes a protectorate of the Ottoman Empire.	The first book in the old Ukrainian language is printed in Kraków and Prague.	Battle of Orsha: Ruthenian army led by Kostiantyn Ostrozkyi beats the Muscovite-German alliance.	Great Khan's Mosque in Bakhchysarai, Crimea is built.	The Zaporizhian Sich is set up on an island in the Dnipro River.	Union of Lublin.

■ 1709	■ 1744	■ 1772–95	■ 1775	■ 1783	■ 1784–1801	■ 1795
Swedish–Cossack forces defeated at Poltava, leads to Russian persecution of Hetmanate rights.	Building work begins on St Andrew's Church in Kyiv.	Three Partitions of Poland divide up the Polish-Lithuanian Commonwealth.	Catherine the Great and Potemkin destroy the Zaporizhian Sich.	Russia demolishes mosques in Crimea; Crimean Tatars flee the region.	Kyiv Arsenal fortress built.	Territories of western Ukraine divided between the Austrian and Russian empires.

■ 1876	■ 1898	■ 1899	■ 1901	■ 1908	■ 1910	■ 1914
Tsar Alexander II bans the Ukrainian language.	The first Trypillian archaeological site is uncovered in the Kyiv region.	City Museum of Antiques and Arts, now the National Art Museum of Ukraine, was opened.	First art school founded in Kyiv.	Davyd Burliuk organizes the Lanka exhibition in Kyiv.	Oleksandr Murashko's works are exhibited at the Venice Biennale.	Kyiv's first independent modern art exhibition, Kiltse.

■ 1922	■ 1928	■ 1932–33	■ 1937	■ 1943	■ 1944	■ Late 1950s
Ukrainian Soviet Socialist Republic formed as part of the Soviet Union.	Stalin's First Five Year Plan begins.	Holodomor famine genocide.	Many artists, including Mykhailo Boichuk and Ivan Padalka, are executed in Stalinist purges.	The Red Army liberates Kyiv from the Nazis.	Stalin deports 250,000 Crimean Tatars.	Khrushchev Thaw slightly loosens political and cultural repression in the Soviet Union.

■ 1993	■ 1994	■ 2000–1	■ 2004	■ 2004	■ 2004	■ 2005
Curator Marta Kuzma comes to Kyiv to direct the new Kyiv Soros Centre for Contemporary Art.	Kuchma becomes president; Budapest Memorandum signed and Ukraine gives up its nuclear arms and other missiles.	Kuchma is exposed for corruption, electoral fraud, and ordering the death of a journalist.	Viktor Yanukovych, supported by Kuchma and Putin, wins the presidential election; Orange Revolution protests claim the election was rigged.	Opposition leader Viktor Yuschenko survives an assassination attempt by dioxin poisoning.	The Orange Revolution leads to a second election, which Yuschenko wins.	Mystetskyi Arsenal, one of the largest exhibition spaces in Europe, is created.

■ 2014	■ 2014	■ 2016	■ 2017	■ 2019	■ 2021	■ 2022
Maidan Revolution: more than 100 killed at protests; Yanukovych flees to Russia, is removed from power, and charged with mass murder of protesters.	In March, Russia illegally annexes Crimea, resulting in war in the Donbas region. In May, Petro Poroshenko is elected as president.	Russia carries out a cyberattack on Kyiv's power grid, causing a major blackout.	Another cyberattack targets the National Bank of Ukraine and the power grid.	Former actor Volodymyr Zelenskyi is elected president with a landslide majority.	April: Russia sends 100,000 troops to the Ukrainian border for 'military exercises'. December: Putin asks NATO to ban Ukraine from membership.	February 24: Russian forces begin invading and attacking Ukrainian territory.

About the Contributors

Andrey Kurkov

Andrey Kurkov is Ukraine's most acclaimed living novelist and author of *Death and the Penguin*. He is also a journalist, prominent public commentator, and current president of PEN Ukraine. Andrey was born in St Petersburg in 1961; his family moved to Kyiv when he was two. After graduating from the Kyiv Foreign Languages Institute (now the Kyiv National Linguistic University), Andrey turned his hand to journalism before serving as a prison guard in Odesa during his military service. A distinguished career as a writer of screenplays and novels followed; more than 150,000 copies of *Death and the Penguin* sold in Ukraine alone, while Andrey's works have been translated into forty-one languages.

Andriy Puchkov

Andriy Puchkov was born in Kyiv and is an architecture specialist, culturologist, art critic, and researcher of art culture. His areas of expertise cover the poetics of ancient architecture, the political history of the Byzantine Empire, the history of classical philology in Ukraine in the nineteenth and twentieth centuries, the theory and history of printing, poetry, Ukrainian drama, and twentieth-century Soviet architecture. Andriy has written more than twenty books and 750 publications on these topics. He is also an Academician of the Ukrainian Academy of Architecture, laureate of the State Prize of Ukraine in the Field of Architecture, and Professor at the Department of Theory and History of Art at the National Academy of Fine Arts and Architecture.

Christian Raffensperger

Christian Raffensperger is Kenneth E. Wray Chair of the Humanities at Wittenberg University, as well as a professor and chair of the History Department. His scholarly work has focused on the integration of the kingdom of Rus specifically, and eastern Europe broadly, into the wider medieval European world. That focus has resulted in books such as *Reimagining Europe: Kievan Rus' in the Medieval World* and *Conflict, Bargaining, and Kinship Networks in Medieval Eastern Europe*, as well as numerous other books and articles.

Diana Klochko

Diana Klochko is a prominent art historian and author of 65 *Masterpieces of Ukrainian Art*. Born in Kozyn village in Ukraine's Rivne oblast, she studied at the National Academy of Visual Arts and Architecture (NAOMA) in Kyiv. Since then, Diana has held various teaching posts, worked as a correspondent and editor, and sat on a number of competition juries; along with a colleague, she founded the Metaphora Translation Award in 2011. Providing specialist advice to art publishers, Diana has also delivered public lectures on the history of art since 2011, as well as curating exhibitions and co-founding the Ukrainian Visual Book Platform. She is a Member of the Ukrainian Section of the International Association of Art Critics AICA (UNESCO) and PEN Ukraine.

Maksym Yaremenko

Maksym Yaremenko is Professor at the Department of History at the National University of Kyiv Mohyla Academy. He is also editor-in-chief of *Kyivska Academia* journal and Senior Researcher at the National Museum of the History of Ukraine. Makysm's fields of interest lie in early modern and modern church history and the history of religious culture, literacy, and education. His most recent book is *Facing the Challenges of Unification and Discipline: The Kyiv Orthodox Metropolitanate in the 18th Century*, published in Ukrainian in 2017.

Alisa Lozhkina

Alisa Lozhkina is an independent art critic and curator from Kyiv and currently based in the US. Between 2013 and 2017 Alisa served as Deputy Director and Chief Curator at Mystetskyi Arsenal, the largest museum and exhibition complex in Ukraine. From 2010 to 2016 she worked as editor-in-chief at major Ukraine art magazine *ART UKRAINE*. Alisa has curated numerous art projects in Ukraine and abroad and written several books, including *Permanent Revolution: Art in Ukraine, XX–early XXI century*, which was published in Ukrainian in 2019 and translated into English and French.

Myroslava M. Mudrak

Myroslava Maria Mudrak is Professor Emeritus of Art History at the Ohio State University and a member of the National Academy of Arts of Ukraine, specializing in eastern European, Ukrainian, and Russian Modernist art in the late nineteenth and early twentieth centuries. Her exhibition catalogue, *Staging the Ukrainian Avant-Garde of the 1910s and 1920s*, was recognized by the 2016 Alfred H. Barr, Jr. Award, while Mudrak's recent publication on Ukraine's premier modern graphic designer, *The Imaginative World of Heorhii Narbut and the Making of a Ukrainian Brand* (2020), has been translated into multiple languages.

Oleksandr Soloviev

Oleksandr Soloviev is an eminent art critic and curator. He graduated from the Kyiv State Art Institute before completing his postgraduate studies at the Institute of Art History of the National Academy of Sciences of Ukraine. Since then, Oleksandr has overseen and curated a number of prominent projects and exhibitions, including at the PinchukArtCentre. In 2015, Oleksandr was

Acknowledgments

the curator and jury member of an exhibition-competition for young Ukrainian and British artists, UK/RAINE, which took place at London's Saatchi Gallery; in 2003, 2007, and 2013, he curated the Ukrainian pavilion at the Venice Biennale. Oleksandr has written for a number of art publications, mainly on topics relating to contemporary Ukrainian art.

Victoria Burlaka
Victoria Burlaka is an art critic and curator specializing in contemporary art in Ukraine. She lives and works in Kyiv; since 2002 she has been a researcher at the Modern Art Research Institute at the National Art Museum of Ukraine. In 2007–2012, Victoria was curator at the Small Gallery of Art Arsenal; between 2009 and 2013 she worked as curator-owner of the Instytutska Gallery in Kyiv; and since 2014, she has been curator of an experimental educational project, the School of Contemporary Art. Victoria is author of several books and articles, including *History of Image: Art of the 2000s* (2011) and *Post-media Optics: Ukrainian Version* (2019).

Thames & Hudson would like to thank the following individuals for generously sharing their time and expertise to bring this book together: Konstantin Akinsha, Ruth Maclennan, Oleksandr Soloviev, and Robert Chandler. Thanks are also due to Andrey Kurkov, Tetyana Teren, and Romana Cacchioli at PEN Ukraine; Burhan Sönmez and Paul Julien at PEN International; Chris Hudson at Motovun; and the Ukrainian Institute in London.

Frank Althaus and Mark Sutcliffe at Fontanka, along with Angus Russell, acted as consultants on the text, as well as fact checking and proofreading the book with meticulous attention and care. Jane Bugaeva and Nina Murray deftly translated multiple chapters, which Peter Dawson laid out. Picture research was undertaken by Sally Nicholls; Fredrika Lokholm assisted with copyright clearances; and Emily Faccini designed the map on pages 12–13. At Thames & Hudson, the team consisted of Sophy Thompson, Tristan de Lancey, Helen Fanthorpe, Kate Mason, and Jane Cutter.

Despite terrible ongoing hardship, galleries and individuals in Ukraine were endlessly helpful in providing images and information for the book. The enviable collections of the Ivan Honchar Museum in Kyiv and the Hutsul Museum in Kolomyia in western Ukraine proved invaluable for the sections on folk art.

Thames & Hudson is immensely grateful to all the book's contributors – Andrey Kurkov, Andriy Puchkov, Christian Raffensperger, Diana Klochko, Maksym Yaremenko, Alisa Lozhkina, Myroslava M. Mudrak, Oleksandr Soloviev, and Victoria Burlaka – for working at speed, often in the most difficult of circumstances.

Thames & Hudson stands in solidarity with the people of Ukraine.

Further Reading

Konstantin Akinsha, *Avant-Garde Betrayed: Kyiv, Kharkiv, Odesa* (London, 2022). A presentation of the groundbreaking art produced in what is now Ukraine in the early twentieth century, accompanying an important exhibition travelling to museums across Europe.

Anne Applebaum, *Red Famine: Stalin's War on Ukraine* (London, 2018). Applebaum's authoritative account of the Holodomor, the man-made famine of 1932–1933 induced by Soviet collectivization in which millions of Ukrainians perished.

Ed. Svitlana Biedarieva, *Contemporary Ukrainian and Baltic Art: Political and Social Perspectives, 1991–2021* (New York, 2021). A deep dive into the transformation that the art scenes of Ukraine, Estonia, Lithuania, and Latvia have undergone since their independence in 1991.

Diana Klochko, *65 Masterpieces of Ukrainian Art: Recognized and Unseen* (Kyiv, 2019). Renowned art critic Klochko reveals the most important artworks in the leading museums of Kyiv, Lviv, Odesa, Kharkiv, and Khmelnytskyi.

Andrey Kurkov, *Ukraine Diaries: Dispatches from Kiev* (London, 2014). Almost out-of-date as soon as it was published, Kurkov's first-hand account of Ukraine's political crisis – beginning with the first day of pro-European protests in November 2013 – gives great insight into life in a country in the midst of profound upheaval and unrest.

Ed. Olena Martynyuk, *Painting in Excess: Kyiv's Art Revival, 1985–1993* (New Brunswick, 2021). This exhibition catalogue, published in partnership with the Zimmerli Art Museum, charts the daring new art produced in Kyiv around the time of the fall of the Soviet Union.

Serhii Plokhy, *The Gates of Europe: A History of Ukraine* (London, 2016). A definitive history of Ukraine by an award-winning Harvard Professor.

Christian Raffensperger, *Reimagining Europe: Kievan Rus' in the Medieval World* (Cambridge, 2012). Raffensperger's important work challenges scholarship that places Kievan Rus' as part of a distinct Byzantine commonwealth, and instead understands Rus' within the wider context of medieval Europe.

Oleksandr Soloviev, *Premonition: Ukrainian Art Now* (London, 2014). Soloviev offers a broad introduction to Ukraine's rousing contemporary art scene, introducing a number of key artists.

Anna Reid, *Borderland: A Journey Through the History of Ukraine* (London, 2015). The updated edition of Reid's 1997 original covers the Euromaidan Revolution of 2014 and the start of the Donbass crisis. A mixture of history and travelogue makes this a digestible introduction to Ukraine's past.

Richard Sakwa, *Frontline Ukraine: Crisis in the Borderlands* (London, 2022). A new and accessible exploration of the origins, history, developments, and global significance of the ongoing war in Ukraine.

Timothy Snyder, *The Reconstruction of Nations: Poland, Ukraine, Lithuania, Belarus, 1569–1999* (New Haven, 2004). Bestselling author Snyder discusses the emergence of Ukrainian, Polish, Lithuanian, and Belarusian nationhood over four centuries.

Serhy Yekelchyk, *Ukraine: Birth of a Modern Nation* (Oxford, 2007). Yekelchyk's history of Ukraine offers unparalleled coverage of the Orange Revolution and its aftermath, exploring modern Ukrainian identity in the post-Soviet era.

Sources of Quotations

p. 154 'In 1909, Murashko's painting *Carousel*...' Zhbankova, Olha. *Oleksandr Murashko. Works from the collection of the National Art Museum of Ukraine.* Kyiv: PC World Ukraine, 2000.

p. 164 'Burliuk promoted the abandonment of all qualities of 'literariness'. As quoted under D. Burliuk's assumed name, Skirgello, 'Vystavka kartin Zveno,' *Kievlianin*, 30 November 1908, No. 332:3.

p. 208 'In his writings, Mykhailov speaks about this...' Sanduliak, Alina. 'Kharkiv School of Photography: Boris Mikhailov', *ART UKRAINE* (artukraine.com.ua), 26 November 2015.

p. 225 'Art historian Ekaterina Degot called his next period...' Degot, Ekaterina. 'Gifts of a Kleptomaniac', *Regina Gallery Chronical*, Moscow, 1993.

p. 229 'The staged photos and videos of these times...' Soloviev, Oleksandr, 'Photoshock without Photoshop', *Imago*, no. 6, 1998.

Sources of Illustrations

We have endeavoured to credit rights owners where possible. The author and publisher apologize for any omissions or errors which we will be happy to correct in future printings and editions of this book.

a=above, b=below, c=centre, l=left, r=right

37a artyOk/123RF.com; **37b** andreyshevchenko/123RF.com; **19** ezarubina/123RF.com; **67** Alex Ishchenko/123RF.com; **72** Johan10/123RF.com; **92** mistervlad/123RF.com; **90** pillerss/123RF.com; **82** raagoon/123RF.com; **88–89** ronedya/123RF.com; **74–75** slava2271/123RF.com; **2, 78, 93, 94, 96, 125, 127, 155, 179, 185, 188, 199a, 214b** akg-images; **141** akg-images/Elizaveta Becker; **146** Heritage Images/Fine Art Images/akg-images; **132ar** Vadym Cherenko/Alamy Stock Photo; **132al, 132ac** Igor Golovnov/Alamy Stock Photo; **112, 118** Robert Harding/Alamy Stock Photo; **172–173** Mariana Ianovska/Alamy Stock Photo; **104–105** Viktor Onyshchenko/Alamy Stock Photo; **131** Panther Media GmbH/Alamy Stock Photo; **97** Prisma by Dukas Presseagentur GmbH/Alamy Stock Photo; **14** Oleksandr Rupeta/Alamy Stock Photo; **139, 193** Maxal Tamor/Alamy Stock Photo; **152** Ivan Vdovin/Alamy Stock Photo; **63** Cambridge University Library; **228** © Ilya Chichkan; **57** Museo Nazionale Archaeologico, Cividale; **230** Photo Marc Domage. Courtesy of the artist and Galleria Continua; **64–65** © Dudlajzov/Dreamstime.com; **169b** © Enigmaart/Dreamstime.com; **68–69** © Gerasimovvv/Dreamstime.com; **86–87** © Kobets/Dreamstime.com; **6–7, 147** © Kateryna Levchenko/Dreamstime.com; **130** © Roman Melnyk/Dreamstime.com; **126** © Serhii Nikolaienko/Dreamstime.com; **121** © Shico300/Dreamstime.com; **120** © Oleksandr Tkachenko/Dreamstime.com; **116–117** © Viacheslav Tykhanskyi/Dreamstime.com; **169a** © Vladwitty/Dreamstime.com; **26–27** © Andrii Zhezhera/Dreamstime.com; **54** Godong/Universal Images Group/Getty Images; **132cc** Igor Golovnov/SOPA Images/LightRocket/Getty Images; **235** © Alexander Gnilitsky (transcribed in the book as Oleksandr Hnylytskyi); **225** © Oleg Holosiy; **124** istockphoto.com; **231** © Nikita Kadan; **8–9, 148, 170** Kharkiv Art Museum; **106–7, 242–3** Yosafat Kobrynskyi National Museum of Hutsulshchyna and Pokuttia Folk Art, Kolomyia; **44, 45, 47** The Bohdan and Varvara National Museum of Arts, Kyiv;

20–21, 48–49, 77, 107br, 132cl, 132cr, 132bl, 132bc, 132br, 133, 160–161, 186–187, 214a, 215a, 215b, 244–5 Ivan Honchar Museum, Kyiv; **18, 99** Manuscript Institute of the VI Vernadsky National Library of Ukraine, Kyiv; **100** Museum of Book and Printing of Ukraine, Kyiv; **162, 174, 175, 176, 177** Museum of Theatrical, Musical and Film Arts of Ukraine, Kyiv; **197** Museum of Ukrainian Art, Kyiv; **73** Collection of the National Museum "Kyiv Art Gallery" (the Kyiv National Art Gallery), **71, 122, 142l, 149, 150–151, 178, 184, 195** National Art Museum of Ukraine, Kyiv. Photo by Mykhailo Andreyev; **156** National Art Museum of Ukraine, Kyiv. Photo by Igor Tyshenko; **153, 196** National Art Museum of Ukraine, Kyiv. Unknown photographer; **5, 22, 29, 30, 31, 32, 33, 34, 35, 41, 60, 61, 70, 166** The National Museum of the History of Ukraine, Kyiv; **134, 142r** Collection of National Museum of Taras Shevchenko, Kyiv; **76** National Museum of Ukraine Folk Decorative Art, Kyiv; **145** Collection of Kyiv Painting Gallery; **181** Private Collection, Kyiv; **103** Sheremetievs Museum, Kyiv. Photo Antikvar Publishing House; **204** © Valeriy Lamakh; **43** Photo Radosław Liwoch (Archaeological Museum in Kraków); **62** British Museum, London; **201** © Anatoliy Lymarev; **183, 206** Borys Voznytskyi Lviv National Art Gallery; **240** © Yarema Malashchuk and Roman Khimei; **220** © Pavlo Markov/Photo Yevhen Nikiforov; **210** © Boris Mihailov. Courtesy of the Artist; **158–59** Collection of the Novakivsky Family; **157** Museum of Odesa Modern Art; **200** Odesa Museum of Fine Arts; **207** NT Art Gallery, Odesa; **209** © Evgeniy Pavlov; **16** © Maria Primachenko; **203** Private collection. © Hrygoly Havrylenko; **199b** Private Collection. © Mykola Hluschenko; **239** © Vlada Ralko; **241** © Danii Rekovsky and Andrey Rachinsky; **232** © REP Group; **223** © Oleksandr Roytburd. Courtesy Betty Roytburd; **227** © Arsen Savadov; **171** Digital image, The Museum of Modern Art, New York/Scala, Florence; **180** Photo The Philadelphia Museum of Art/Art Resource/Scala, Florence; © Alexander Archipenko Foundation; **85** Ruslan Lytvyn/Shutterstock; **212** manhattan_art/Shutterstock; **39** Ovchinnikova Irina/Shutterstock; **115** rbrechko/Shutterstock; **237** © Tibery Silvashi; **50, 58, 91** National Library of Russia, St Petersburg; **108, 119** Photo Mykola Swarnyk CC BY-SA 3.0; **216, 224** © Oleg Tistol; **236** © Vasiliy Tsagalov; **129** Visnyk CC BY-SA 4.0; **233** © Stanislov Volyazlovsky; **101** Ostroh Castle Museum, Volyn; **59** Valery Yotov; **205** © Karlo Zvirynsky.

Index

Testament

When I die, then bury me
On a rolling plain.
Raise my barrow in the soil
Of my dear Ukraine
With the wheatfields and the cliffs
Of a plunging shore
In my sight, where I can hear
The booming Dnipro's roar.

When its seaward waters bear
The invaders' blood
From Ukraine, then I will leave
Field and hill for good.
I will quit it all and fly
Bursting up to God
And say prayers...but till then
I don't know a god.

Taras Shevchenko
Translated by A.Z. Foreman, 2022

This is a translated extract from Taras Shevchenko's original version of 'Testament' ('Zapovit'), 1845. Though Ukraine has produced numerous prominent poets and writers, especially in the twentieth century – Isaac Babel, Mykhail Bulgakov, and Anatoly Kuznetsov, among others – Taras Shevchenko stands out as the nation's greatest literary figure. Shevchenko dedicated his life to Ukrainian self-determination and his work continues to resonate today, inspiring contemporary poets, writers, and translators to produce works in his honour.